FEED MY SHEEP

Sermons on Contemporary Issues in Pastoral Care

GREGORY J. JOHANSON,
editor

PAULIST PRESS
New York/Ramsey

The Publisher gratefully acknowledges the use of excerpts from *Monsignor Quixote,* copyright © 1982 by Graham Greene, reprinted by permission of Simon & Schuster, Inc.

Library of Congress
Catalog Card Number: 83-61995

ISBN: 0-8091-2593-5

Published by Paulist Press
545 Island Road, Ramsey, N.J. 07446

Printed and bound in the
United States of America

CONTENTS

Postscript

ACKNOWLEDGEMENTS

Grateful acknowledgement is made to the following for permission to use previously published material: "Insight and Availability," a sermonic condensation from *Creative Ministry* by Henri J. M. Nouwen, copyright 1971 by Henri J. M. Nouwen, and reprinted by permission of Doubleday and Company, Inc.; "Aging and Caring," a sermonic condensation from *Aging* by Henri J. M. Nouwen and Walter J. Gaffney, copyright 1974 by Henri J. M. Nouwen and Walter J. Gaffney, and reprinted by permission of Doubleday and Company, Inc.; "The Obstacle of Doublemindedness," a sermonic presentation of some material contained in "Dealing with Double-Mindedness" by William E. Hulme, copyright 1982 by William E. Hulme, and reprinted by permission of Harper and Row; "The Advent of Giants" first published in modified form as "Raising the Giant Within You" by Gregory J. Johanson in *Pulpit Resource*, Vol. 5, 3rd Quarter, 1977, No. 3, reprinted by permission of the author; Excerpts from *The Jerusalem Bible*, copyright 1966 by Darton Longman and Todd, Ltd. and Doubleday and Company, Inc., are used by permission of the publisher; Scriptural quotations noted RSV are from the *Revised Standard Version of the Bible*, copyrighted 1946, 1952, 1971, 1973 by the Division of Christian Education of the National Council of Churches of Christ in the U.S.A. and are used by permission.

Special thanks to Mrs. Martin Weber for her gracious and invaluable help in typing the final manuscript.

*This volume is dedicated
to the staff of the Georgia
Association For Pastoral
Care who incarnate in their
healing ministries the
spirit of Christ's command,
"Feed my sheep."*

PREFACE

In one of our first meetings, about twelve years ago, I recall telling Greg Johanson that he was a lonely young man who had found Hope. Like many other things we said to each other during the years he was studying in Atlanta, this had both a literal and a symbolic meaning. Greg had found Hope, his wife, a person who complemented his personality in a significant way. He had also found Hope in the Christian message and in the church, which would, as he struggled to see how it fit his own life and need, continue to enrich his calling to ministry. Greg was one of those persons, more fortunate than most, who became aware of his need for pastoral care early in life. He was willing to ask for help in putting his personal pain and hope together and to give some of us an opportunity to be his pastor, supervisor, and teacher. If pastoral care centers, such as ours, have anything like a "full service customer," Greg was one of them.

Since he left Atlanta in the early 1970's, a major concern of his ministry had been to integrate clinical training with his work as a parish minister. His article, "The Parish Revisited: Reflections on How CPE Helped and Hindered a Return to Parish Ministry after Training" (*The Journal of Pastoral Care*, Vol. XXXII, September 1978, No. 3, pp. 147–154), reveals both the contributions of the specialized pastoral care ministry to the min-

1

istry of the parish and some of the continuing tension between them. At the time of writing that article, Greg saw in his CPE experience "a de-emphasis on preaching," and took as part of his vocation bringing preaching and pastoral care together—a task which is carried out in this volume. Greg believes, as do I, that "all ministers, generalists and specialists alike, are about the same basic task of theology," whether that theological reflection takes place in a sermon or in the interpretive word given in pastoral care and counseling.

The purpose of this book, as I see it, is twofold: (1) to bring the functions of preaching and of pastoral care closer together into a more unified ministry, and (2) to offer the continuing good news that in the midst of the pain of life, we too can find Hope.

John Patton
The Georgia Association for Pastoral Care

EDITOR'S INTRODUCTION

GENERAL MINISTRY
AND THE CHRISTIAN IMAGINATION

Ministers with a special concern and expertise in pastoral care and counseling function toward the same general end as all ministers and theologians do. They are about the business of cultivating what Ted Jennings has called "the Christian Imagination."[1] No person experiences the world just as it is. The world is made available to our consciousness only through the active work of our imaginations which filter and structure all the sensations that impinge on us. Our experience of the world then makes sense to us, has meaning, and we are able to move about, communicate, and be oriented within it.

Differing imaginations lead to differing understandings and experience of the same event, as when one person stiffens in fear at the thought of putting his/her arm around others while singing in Sunday service while another melts in gratitude at the same

---

1. See *Introduction to Theology* by Theodore W. Jennings, Jr., Fortress Press, Philadelphia, 1976 for a good overview of the phenomenological structure of theological thought and practice common to both liberal and conservative traditions.

thought. Imaginations can become distorted so that they function not to open up new, expanded, nourishing experiences but rather to close down or hurtfully limit experience and expression of life.

Christian pastors and theologians are committed to the Judeo-Christian heritage and to how the various elements of its tradition color our imaginations and make life available to us. They believe that if a person is grasped and encountered by the tradition in a living way, that will bring to expression the experience of the Sacred in life for them and make life available in its truest, more meaningful, and authentic forms. For instance, it makes a concrete, passionate, historical difference how one sees a stranger. One may perceive a threat. Through the filters of the mind of Christ and the Scriptures, one may perceive instead a fellow traveler, pilgrim, brother or sister in Christ. The difference is not in the world, but in our interpretation of the world.

In their practice then, all ministers, generalists and specialists alike, are about the same basic task of theology, that of interpreting and applying the various canonical images, symbols, parables, narratives, etc., to their particular historical day and time, attempting to make them available to contemporary consciousness. This is true whether the pastor is counseling somebody one to one or preaching on Sunday morning. The methods may differ, but the task is the same—that of healing or cultivating the imaginations of persons whose fundamental way of experiencing and expressing themselves in the world has either become distorted or is yet underdeveloped.

The underlying faith is that if we all had the freedom of experience and expression in life that the Scriptures seek to open up, we would experience life in a self-authenticating way as good, and be reconciled with ourselves and our neighbors. We would be participating in the power to be, becoming all that we could be and making our world all that God intends it to be.

Since all our self-understandings are not so-colored, the church continues to exist as a community dedicated to carrying out Christ's command to "Feed my sheep," to giving people what they need in order to find nourishment and enjoyment in life and spontaneously praise God in thanksgiving.

There are many realms in which this command is carried out. Pastoral care had generally attended to the realm of the personal and interpersonal in a special way. Since this is a volume of sermons on traditional pastoral care issues, the reader will find particular themes of the Christian Imagination underlined and carried as threads through the book. These themes generally revolve around the issues of how people cut themselves off from the goodness of creation which is realistically available to them because of their distorted or limited way of being in the world. Sermons which are oriented toward changing political, economic, or social consciousness so that people are not limited by external forces involve a different complimentary realm of pastoral concern.

Five traditional themes can be identified in particular in the following pages: (1) "There is one God and Maker of us all" generally interpreted in terms of saying we are all in this together, we are more alike than different, or there are no strong people vs. weak people, no good guys vs. bad guys in the world. (2) "God's creation is good" (Gen 1:31) understood in terms of saying we have what it takes, we do not need a new humanity, we are the salt of the earth, the light of the world. (3) "Sin" expounded as alienation and separation from God's original goodness in us, and as our temptation to play God by attempting to create a world more to our liking and less frightening than the realities we have been given. (4) "Salvation" or "redemption" communicated as a matter of accepting the grace of God which deems us worthwhile and lovable, and frees us from our frantic, hurtful, unproductive attempts to manufacture our own basis for acceptance in the world. (5) "God is with us," "Jesus is Emmanuel," which is seen in affirmations that growth is possible, reconciliation, healing, and greater wholeness can happen. These five themes provide a foundation or backdrop that is sensed throughout pastoral care activities in general[2] and these sermons in particular, even when they are not being explicitly expounded by name.

---

2. Confer G. Johanson, "The Parish Revisited," *The Journal of Pastoral Care*, Vol. XXXII, September 1978, No. 3.

HEALING THE IMAGINATION: A PREDICAMENT

When someone's mind, basic filters, or imagination, through which one experiences and expresses oneself in the world, has rigidified, causing a distorted, truncated, painful perception of life, a real challenge is presented to Christian ministry that intends to be about the business of healing.

The church, in general, with its historic tools of preaching and sacrament, and the pastoral care and counseling movement, in particular, with its new arsenal of modern psychotherapies, are in closer agreement about this predicament in the 1980's than they were a few decades earlier.[3] There was a period when pastors who were disenchanted with the power and effectiveness of preaching and ritual to bring about change gravitated to the psychology and therapy of the twentieth century. They hoped that in the intensity and dynamics of interpersonal encounter, the power of the gospel might be manifest. Today there are ample studies to call into question, statistically at least, the relative efficiency of either mode to effect change in persons. On the other hand, there are a wealth of anecdotal examples that clearly commend the power of both preaching and counseling to meaningfully touch human lives. The general result is that "preachers" and "counselors" now have a healthy measure of both humility and respect in relation to each other, which must be taken as a good sign for Christianity in the 1980's and beyond.

Part of the overall common predicament is becoming clear. Modern learning theory has underlined much ancient wisdom in delineating at least two different processes that affect one's imagination. One process has been termed "accommodating." Accommodating is the process of changing or adjusting mental pictures or filters to include new information, new experiences, data that enlarges our minds and knowledge. A child's mind must be doing a lot of this throughout the child's development, as in expanding the concept of "daddy" when it is found that more than one male figure in this world corresponds and responds to this designation.

---

3. Confer John H. Patton, "Pastoral Counseling Comes of Age," *The Christian Century*, March 4, 1981.

The other process is called "assimilating." Assimilating is a process in which we take in new experiences and modify them to make them fit with what we already know, whether it is a good fit or not. As adults, we tend to be more rigid and unyielding than children, to hear and see more of what we want to hear and see, to do more assimilating than accommodating. And on one level, that is good. We are not thrown to and fro by every new doctrine, fad, or friend who comes along. On the other hand we have the challenge this section started with.

How can a preacher or a counselor helpfully communicate with someone who is rigidly and hurtfully assimilating, distorting information and experience, including any liberating message that might be offered?

Again, through a confluence of modern knowledge and almost forgotten ancient wisdom, some of the answers to the above question are beginning to emerge.

Number one, it is becoming more evident that a slight shift in consciousness has to happen in worship or counseling. We normally go around in our everyday ordinary consciousness ruled by habits and routines, not allowing the possibility of anything new, even if that newness is precisely what we are needing. "We have all sinned" as the Scriptures say, and we are now caught in it, as Paul points out; we are seeing through a glass darkly.

The need to cultivate a different, non-ordinary consciousness is something that the church and counselors have recognized intuitively for aeons. We go to a sanctuary, office or retreat site set apart. We are provided with a different setting, a silence, a type of music, practice, or task, designed to help us get out of normal gear into a more neutral state. There our minds and hearts can be more easily accessed, more receptive, more open to the surprises the Sacred might have for us. In the history of the church this state of consciousness has been termed prayerful, meditative, or worshipful consciousness. In contemporary and Eastern counseling it is sometimes called experiential or witnessing consciousness. By either name there is a quality of openness that is missing from the ordinary consciousness we normally mobilize to go to the grocery store. Of course, the ordinary consciousness that we take to the store is generally the most appropriate one. We need to have our routines and habits. It is not helpful to meditate on how to push in a clutch and shift gears in busy traffic.

There also needs to be a quality of mystery in this shift in consciousness that is often missing in both worship and the counseling office today. Mystery means something is not nailed down, or not colored in solid as far as the imagination is concerned. For instance, we might see someone coming down the street in our neighborhood going toward the post office. At first we might not know who it is. So we are open. We allow the answer to emerge and to teach us. Our not knowing provides the possibility of learning, of looking with fresh eyes. But as soon as we think we know and label the experience, it is all over. "Oh yeah, that's Rev. Avery. Comes down here all the time to get his mail." Thud! The gate is closed. We assimilate the experience into what we think we know and close the doors on the possibility of anything novel. Rev. Avery's color is green, he is always such and such, and is not expected to be anything else. So today when he comes out of the post office we don't notice something new about him. His mouth is slightly down. He might be sad, might have received some unhappy news. But we tend not to notice.

It is deadly in a church service if a minister gets up to preach on a familiar parable and the response is, "Oh yeah. I know that one. Heard it a thousand times." Or perhaps the minister has been there over a year and the response is, "Oh yeah. Here he goes into his routine again." There is then no sense of mystery that could open the door to the mind's being colored with new possibilities. Similarly, if a counselor brings someone's awareness to an area by commenting, "A little sad, huh," and the response is in an ordinary conversational vein, "Oh yeah, well, I always get a little sad toward the end of the month when bills are due," there is not much possibility of new insight. It is a different situation if the person responds with curiosity and accepts an invitation to simply be with the experience for a period and see if its meaning becomes any clearer over time. It is a different situation in worship if the response is, "You know, he didn't really do that passage the way I thought, and that makes me wonder."

A second point that is becoming clear about the process of accessing someone's core organizing beliefs through an opening of consciousness is that there must be a high degree of trust, safety, and security provided.

That brings everything back to the person of the healer. The preacher or the counselor must ultimately be a safe and trustworthy presence, and be experienced as such by the particular person or people being ministered to. It is a simple fact that people are not going to open themselves and drop their defenses if they feel threatened or unsafe. If they feel that someone is up to something, that something is being put over on them, or that they are being judged, manipulated, or condemned, they will automatically mobilize to defend and protect themselves.[4]

The good news that we are justified by grace takes this reality into account and instills in the healer the necessary quality of unconditional acceptance. The knowledge of the love from which we cannot be separated, the love which casts out all fear, is alone able to open a painful, hurtful imagination to new possibilities. And it is no simple matter to creatively incarnate that gracefulness over a long enough period that it is perceived and accepted by suspicious and rigid persons. Wisdom, skill, and the intangible power of the Spirit need to be added, but the graciousness, humanity, and trustworthiness of the preacher and the counselor are the foundation on which meaningful change must build.

It is these qualities in the relationship of the preacher to the congregation, the trust and respect that are there, the degree to which an open and receptive quality of consciousness has been engendered, that are difficult to evaluate in the printed sermons of this volume. The reader can experiment with his or her own experience by willfully projecting a poor opinion on an author and reading fast, and then assuming good will and reading with anticipation and respect.

The pages preceding each sermon offer some specifics about the content and context in which it was delivered, along with some brief notes on the person preaching. This is intended to help

---

4. Confer *Hakomi Therapy*, by Ron Kurtz, Hakomi Institute, P.O. Box 1873, Boulder, Colorado 80306, 1983, for a discussion of safety issues plus witnessing states of consciousness as applied by counseling situations.

bridge part of the vacuum created by the necessity of transplanting live, historical events to static pages of print.

PERSONS, CONTENTS, CONTEXTS

In addition to the content of a sermon, what contributes to its being termed "pastoral" is the person of the minister and the context within which he or she is speaking. The many contributors to this volume present various styles, moods, and modes of presentation in their works, reflecting once again the truth of Phillip Brooks' statement that preaching is "truth through personality"—a consistent state of affairs for an historical religion stressing the incarnation of the Spirit.

None of the sermons in this volume have been edited to cut out the indications of a specific, concrete, historical occasion. They were all "oral events" before being committed to paper for publication. Their oral character has been retained in the belief, continuously held up by pastoral theology in general, that the particular and universal must be kept in tension in theological reflection. Ted Jennings argues historically and biblically that the Christian Imagination is actually delineated by the forms of time, the concrete and definite, and the passionate.

The contributors for this volume are all pastors who have a special expertise or sensitivity in the area of pastoral care and counseling. The total group is comprised of pastors in local churches, in specialized pastoral care and counseling facilities, and in institutions of higher learning. The broad spectrum is represented within which professional pastoral care and counseling is happening today.

All of the sermons in this volume represent attempts to be faithful to Christ's command: "Feed my sheep." They seek to cultivate the Christian Imagination through the spoken word in relation to traditional areas of concern for pastoral care.

Gregory J. Johanson
Advent 1982

Principles

INSIGHT AND AVAILABILITY
Henri J. M. Nouwen

Henri J. M. Nouwen is one of the leading voices in the pas-toral care movement today. His close integration of profes-sional and spiritual-personal issues, as well as the evocative images that his writings offer, has struck responsive chords in many pastors. His particular works included in this volume are condensed, sermonic versions of expanded works origi-nally published in book form.

In *Insight and Availability*, which first appeared in expanded form in his book *Creative Ministry* published by Doubleday & Company, Garden City, New York, 1971, Nouwen outlines some of the obstacles that prevent preaching from leading to life-changing insight. He considers the person of the preacher who might work through these barriers. He underlines the necessity of the ones who speak to be genuinely available to themselves and to others through dialogue. Only then can they hope for their congregation to progress in the pilgrimage of becoming human according to the model of Christ.

INTRODUCTION

In 1857 Anthony Trollope wrote in *Barchester Towers:* "There is, perhaps, no greater hardship at present inflicted on mankind in civilized and free countries, than the necessity of listening to sermons." (Cf. *U.S. Catholic,* July 1970, "Let's Abolish the Sun-day Sermon," by Daphne D. C. Pochin Mould.) I would not be surprised to find many people today who are willing to agree with him.

The more amazing it is, therefore, that there are still so many preachers who want to preach and so many people who are willing to listen. Why is this so? Perhaps because people today, just as much as a century ago, have a lasting desire to come to such an insight in their own condition and the condition of their world, they can be free to follow Christ: that is, to live their lives just as authentically as He lived His. The purpose of preaching is none other than to help people come to this basic insight.

Insight is more than intellectual understanding—it is knowledge through and through, knowledge to which the whole person can say Yes. It is an understanding that pervades people from head to heart, from top to toe, from brain to guts. When people can come to this totally permeating knowledge, they will be able to really listen to the Word of God and to follow the light that entered into their darkness. In this way, one of the most crucial purposes of preaching is to remove these real and all-too-visible obstacles that cause people to listen without understanding.

It would be extremely presumptuous to even try to touch the many aspects of preaching. Therefore, I would like to limit myself to just one question: "What kind of person is it who can help take away those obstacles that prevent the Word of God from falling on fertile ground?"

Redundancy of the message and fear of the Truth seem to be two basic reasons why preachers have such difficulty in coming close to their audiences. Before we can ask what kind of person will be able to break through this deep-seated human-listener resistance against the message, we have to be honest enough to confess that it is not just the message but also the messengers themselves who often keep people away from painful but liberating insights. Let us, therefore, now examine the problem of the messenger.

I

THE PROBLEM OF THE MESSENGER

Many preachers tend to increase the resistance against listening instead of decreasing it by the way in which they tend to get their eternal message across.

1. Non-Existent Feelings

A large number of sermons start by making untested suppositions. Without any hesitance, many preachers impose feelings, ideas, questions, and problems on their hearers that are often completely unknown to the majority, if not to all of them.

Sometimes whole sermons are built on clerical feelings that are quite alien to laypersons. I remember one sermon that began as follows:

> Today we all congregate together to celebrate the ascension of our Lord Jesus Christ. Only a few weeks ago our hearts were still filled with joy because of the resurrection of our Lord, and now already we feel with the Apostles the sadness about His leaving us. But let us not despair, because Jesus does not leave us alone but is going to send us the Holy Spirit within a few days.

It came as no surprise to find that everyone was mentally absent by the time the preacher finished his introduction. I counted about thirty people scattered in the big, mostly empty church. Nobody seemed to remember how happy he was at Easter or to realize how sad he was on Ascension Day. There was no congregation, no celebration, no community, certainly no despair or desire to have the Holy Spirit come soon. Just a couple of isolated individuals who had kept in mind that Ascension Day is a day of obligation and were faithful enough to go to Mass.

Even more irritating than this, however, are preachers who somehow seem to know exactly how everybody feels. A good example is the following introduction:

> Brothers and Sisters in Christ: In a time in which we all have become part of the big American rat race, in which we are forced to become victims of our watches and slaves of our agendas, in which we are running from one committee meeting to another, we have become deaf to the voice of God who speaks in silence and reveals himself in the quiet moment of prayer.

Well, this certainly tells us a lot about the preacher—but what about the grandmother who spent a good part of the week solving crossword puzzles, what about the boy who just came back from the baseball field, and his teacher who spent his Saturday reading Dostoyevsky, and what about the housewife who enjoyed a nice afternoon with her kids at the city zoo?

Perhaps someone in the audience might say Yes to the preacher, but most will feel just as far from his words as they feel from the so-called rat race. They might not be aware of this, but in one way or another—by a protective numbness or an outright expression of hostility—they will show that they are not really with him.

2. *Theological Preoccupation*

A second and even more difficult problem to overcome is the theological preoccupation of the preacher. Some preachers become so excited about a recent book they have read or a new viewpoint they have heard that they feel compelled to have others share their enthusiasm. They quickly and, as it often happens, disappointingly find out, however, that Karl Rahner, Harvey Cox, or Schillebeeckx do not appeal as much, if at all, to their hearers as they do to themselves. The main reason is not that their theological ideas are not valid or meaningful, but rather that not only those who preach but also those who listen have their own "theologies." Let me explain this with a story.

A theology student was asked to give a sermon about the Kingdom of God. He carefully studied the Scriptures and read the latest literature on the subject. But when he thought he had a clear idea about the Kingdom of God and was ready to present his sermon, the suggestion was made to him to first visit four families living in the parish where he was going to preach and ask them what they thought about the Kingdom of God.

So he went first to a meteorologist, a scholarly man who had read many books in his life and had discovered that making predictions was a pretty tricky business. And the meteorologist said: "The Kingdom of God is the fulfillment of God's promises, and man has to refrain from the unhealthy curiosity of exactly how this will happen."

Then the student went to a storekeeper, whose business had been a failure and whose wife had been sick for many years. And the storekeeper said: "The Kingdom of God is heaven—where I finally will receive my reward for enduring my hard, bothersome life."

From the storekeeper he went to a wealthy farmer, who had a strong wife and two beautiful and healthy children. And the farmer said: "The Kingdom of God is a beautiful garden where we all will continue the happy life we started in this world."

Finally, the student came to the house of a laborer, who had learned a good trade and was proud that he was able to earn his money with his own hands. And the laborer said: "The Kingdom of God was a smart invention of the Church to keep the illiterate happy and the poor content, but since I can take care of myself and have a good job I have no need anymore for a Kingdom to come."

When the theology student came home from his visits and read his sermon again, he realized suddenly that his ideas were close to those of the meteorologist, who was used to living with uncertainties, but that the storekeeper looking for a reward, the farmer hoping for the continuation of his happiness, and the laborer who saw the Kingdom in the works of his own hands would not understand him. And when he read the Scriptures again he discovered that there was a place for all four of his parishioners in the Kingdom of God. (These data are used with the permission of Mr. Leo Lans, student of Catholic Theological Institute in Utrecht, Holland.)

Perhaps the greatest temptation of preachers is to think that only they have a theology and to believe that the best thing to do is to convert all those who listen to their way of thinking. In this way, however, they have failed to realize that in a very real sense they have not loved their neighbor as themselves, since they have not taken their views and experiences just as seriously as their own. When this is true, in fact, many of those who listen to their viewpoint will become indifferent or irritated without exactly knowing why. And the preachers who spend a great deal of time studying books and preparing their sermons will themselves become more and more disillusioned as they start feeling that nobody wants to listen to the Word of God. All the while, however, they have forgotten that God's Word does not have to be exactly the same as their own. When preachers address themselves to non-existent feelings and are anxiously preoccupied with their own theology, they tend to increase instead of decrease the already existing resistance against the message.

There is no tool, no technique, no special skill which can solve these problems for the preacher. But perhaps there is a "spirituality"—a way of living—that can give hope to the ones who want to bring their people to a liberating insight which can make them free to follow Christ. Let us, therefore, now examine the kind of person who can help others to come to this insight.

II
THE ONE WHO LEADS TO INSIGHT

The task of every preacher is to assist people in their ongoing struggle of becoming. And this is accomplished primarily by speaking about Christ, who lived His life with an increasing willingness to face His own condition and the conditions of the world in which He found Himself, in such a way that people are encouraged to follow Him; that is, to live their life with the same authenticity even if it leads them to tears, sweat, and, possibly, a violent death.

Every preacher is called upon to take away the obstacles that prevent this painful process of humans becoming human. This is a difficult task since there seems to be a profound resistance in man against change, at least when it concerns their basic outlook on life. Once we have a more or less satisfying standpoint, we tend to cling to it since it always seems better to have at least a poor standpoint than to have none at all. In this sense people are basically very conservative. They are constantly tempted to deny their most precious human ability—which is to shift standpoints—and yield easily to their tendency to settle for the comfortable routine. In many ways they are resistant to the call of Him who says that when you are young you can put on your own belt and walk where you like, but when you grow old you will stretch your hands where you would rather not go (John 21:18). In complete contrast to our idea that adulthood means the ability to take care of oneself, Jesus describes it as a growing willingness to stretch out one's hands and be guided by others.

It is no wonder, then, that preachers who hope to remove the obstacles of this process of growth and to have their people become free to surrender themselves and let others gird them are considered persons of great courage.

The two aspects of preaching that seem to be most essential for a preacher to facilitate this ongoing process of becoming arc (1) dialogue and (2) availability.

1. *The Capacity for Dialogue*

When I use the word dialogue I do not think about dialogue homilies in which everyone can say what he or she wants, nor about a public discussion or any other specific technique to make people participate. No, nothing of that is meant by the word dialogue. I simply mean a way of relating to men and women so that they are able to respond to what is said with their own life experience. In this way dialogue is not a technique but an attitude of the preacher who is willing to enter into a relationship in which partners can really influence each other. In a true dialogue the preacher cannot stay on the outside. Preachers cannot remain untouchable and invulnerable. They have to be totally and most personally involved. This can be a completely internal process in which there is no verbal exchange of words, but it requires the risk of real engagement in the relationship between those who speak and those who listen. Only then can we talk about a real dialogue.

When this dialogue takes place, those who listen will come to the recognition of who they really are since the words of the preacher will find a sounding board in their own hearts and find anchor places in their personal life-experiences. And when they allow the words to come so close as to become their flesh and blood, they can say: "What you say loudly, I whispered in the dark; what you pronounce so clearly, I had some suspicion about; what you put in the foreground, I felt in the back of my mind; what you hold so firmly in your hand always slipped away through my fingers. Yes, I find myself in your words because your words come from the depths of human experiences and, therefore, are not just yours but also mine, and your insights do not just belong to you, but are mine as well."

When a man who listens to a preacher can say this, there is a real dialogue. And if he were a little more spontaneous than most of us are, he would say, "Yes, brother, you said it. Yes,

Amen, Alleluia." Only then are persons able to recognize real dialogue and affirm their real selves and come to the confession not only of their deficiencies and mistakes but also of themselves as persons in desperate need for the Word of God which has the power to make them free. But when people are not able to understand what is going on within themselves, when they do not know what they really want, feel, or do, then words that come from above cannot penetrate into the center of their person. When emotions, ideas, and aspirations are cluttered together in an impermeable dirty crust, no dew can bring forth fruits and no clouds can "rain the just."

But whenever anxious and impenetrable people are approached by a fellow human being who expresses solidarity with them and offers personal insight and understanding as a source of recognition and clarification, then their confusion can be taken away and paths that may lead to light can become visible. Then the meteorologist, the storekeeper, the farmer, and the laborer will realize that the person up there is simply taking away the veil that prevented them from seeing not his but their own viewpoints. Then they will recognize that he is speaking about them and that the Word of God is not for him alone.

But again, dialogue is not a technique or special skill you can learn in school, but a way of life. In the final analysis, dialogue can only become actual through a willingness on the part of preachers to be available to their audience in a very basic sense. And so, I would finally like to examine this availability as the core of the spirituality of the preacher.

2. *Availability*

Availability is the primary condition for every dialogue that is to lead to a redemptive insight. Preachers who are not willing to make their understanding of their own faith and doubt, anxiety and hope, fear and joy available as a source of recognition for others can never expect to remove the many obstacles which prevent the Word of God from bearing fruit.

But it is here that we touch precisely upon the spirituality of preachers themselves. In order to be available to others, persons have to be available to themselves first of all. And we know how extremely difficult it is to be available to ourselves, to have our own experiences at our disposal. We know how selective our self-understanding really is. If we are optimists, we are apt to remember those events of the day that tend to reinforce our positive outlook on life. If we are pessimists, we might say to ourselves: "Again, another day that proves that I am no good." But where are the realists who are able to allow all their experiences to be theirs, and to accept their happiness as well as their sadness, their hate as well as their love, as really belonging to their own human experiences? When people do not have all their experiences at their disposal they tend to make only those available to others that fit best the image they want to have of themselves and their world. And this is exactly what we call "closed-mindedness." It is the blindness of people to an essential part of their own reality.

Preachers who want to be real leaders are the ones who are able to put the full range of their life-experiences—their experiences in prayer, in conversation and in their lonely hours—at the disposal of those who ask them to be their preacher. Pastoral care does not mean running around nervously trying to redeem people, to save them at the last moment, or to put them on the right track by a good idea, an intelligent remark, or practical advice. No! People are redeemed once and for all. Pastoral care means in the final analysis: offering your own life-experience to your fellow human beings and, as Paul Simon sings, to lay yourself down like a bridge over troubled water.

I am not saying that you should talk about yourself, your personal worries, your family, your youth, your illnesses, or your hang-ups. That has nothing to do with availability. That is only playing a narcissistic game with your own idiosyncrasies. No, I mean that preachers are called to experience life to such a depth that the meteorologist, the storekeeper, the farmer, and the laborer will all one day or another realize that they are touching places where their own lives also really vibrate, and in this way they allow them to become free to let the Word of God do its redemptive work. Because, as Carl Rogers says: "What is most personal is most general." (*On Becoming a Person,* Houghton Mifflin, New York, 1961, p. 26) Thomas Oden explains this when he writes: "Repeatedly I have found, to my astonishment, that the feelings which have seemed to me most private, most personal, and therefore the feelings I least expect to be understood by others, when clearly expressed, resonate deeply and consistently with their own experience. This has led me to believe that what I experience in the most unique and personal way, if brought to clear expression, is precisely what others are most deeply experiencing in analogous ways." (*The Structure of Awareness,* Abingdon Press, Nashville and New York, 1969, pp. 23–24.)

When people listen to preachers who are really available to them and, therefore, able to offer their own life experience as a source of recognition, they no longer have to be afraid to face their own condition and that of their world because the ones who stand before them are the living witnesses that insight makes them free and does not create new anxieties. Only then can indifference and irritation be removed; only then can the Word of God, which has been repeated so often but understood so little, find fertile ground and be rooted in the soul of humanity.

So we have seen how, through availability, a real dialogue can take place which can lead to new insight. This is to say that the Word of God, which is a sign of contradiction and a sword piercing the heart of humanity, can only reach people when it has become flesh and blood of them who preach it.

THE HEALING PRESENCE
James W. Ewing, Ph.D.

Formerly, James Ewing was a professor of pastoral ministries at Eden Theological Seminary. He moved from that position to become the first and current full-time Executive Director of the American Association of Pastoral Counselors. In this position he travels throughout the United States and speaks in a variety of settings.

The Healing Presence is a sermon by Ewing which outlines the general process of healing that people go through which parallels the experience of Isaiah in the Holy of Holies. In it he maintains the principle that whether a person experiences a healing touch through the mediation of a sermon, a relationship with a pastoral counselor, or a walk in the wilderness, the ultimate source of healing is the presence of God which encounters people as a matter of grace, transcending all human control and manipulation.

God confronts us with his presence and we are healed. This is the witness of generation after generation. In the experience of Isaiah in the Holy of Holies, we are exposed to the power, fear and fullness of the Healing presence of God.

In the year that King Uzziah died I saw the Lord sitting upon a throne, high and lifted up; and his train filled the temple. Above him stood the seraphim; each had six wings: with two he covered his face, and with two he covered his feet, and with two he flew. And one called to another and said: "Holy, holy, holy is the Lord of hosts; the whole earth is full of his glory." And the foundations of the thresholds shook at the voice of him who called and the house was filled with smoke. And I said: "Woe is me! For I am lost; for I am a man of unclean lips, and I dwell in the midst of a people of unclean lips; for my eyes have seen the King, the Lord of hosts!"

Then flew one of the seraphim to me, having in his hand a

burning coal which he had taken with tongs from the altar. And he touched my mouth and said: "Behold, this has touched your lips; your guilt is taken away, and your sin forgiven." And I heard the voice of the Lord saying, "Whom shall I send, and who will go for us?" Then I said, "Here am I! Send me." And he said, "Go, and say to this people:

'Hear and hear, but do not understand; see and see, but do not perceive.'
Make the heart of this people fat, and their ears heavy, and shut their eyes; lest they see with their eyes, and hear with their ears, and understand with their hearts, and turn and be healed."

Then I said, "How long, O Lord?"
And he said:
Until cities lie waste without inhabitant, and houses without men, and the land is utterly desolate, and the Lord removes men far away, and the forsaken places are many in the midst of the land.

(Isaiah 6:1–12 RSV)

The passage opens with the time of deep and significant change in the life of Judah. King Uzziah had died. The respected monarch who had guided and protected the people for forty years was gone. Inside the nation, grief and fear stirred uncertainty. Outside the nation, the strong power of Assyria threatened to invade. Isaiah was stricken with grief and overwhelming confusion as to the meaning of the events of the time. He had gone to the Temple and there he saw the Lord seated on the throne.

An amazing and powerful process began. The Temple was alive with God's presence and the throne with the seraphim breathed the spirit of God with vibrant refrain:

Holy, Holy, Holy, is the Lord of Hosts
The whole earth is full of his Glory.

For Isaiah though, this awesome refrain was painful news. The deep hurt and anxiety of his own imperfection and separation struck like a hammer on an anvil in the pit of his inward parts:

Woe is me! I am lost; for I am a man of unclean lips
And I dwell in the midst of a people of unclean lips;
Yet with these eyes I have seen the King,
The Lord of Hosts!

The realization of lostness, the awareness of isolation from the power of life, the vivid array of self-deception blazed with overwhelming fear of annihilation. The incongruity between the inward awareness and the vision of the profound holiness and fullness of God spun around in him with devastating power. Helplessness surrounds him, paralyzed by the realization that any movement only intensified the pain of lostness.

Then an amazing change occurred as the seraph moved into that unbridgeable gap carrying in his hand a burning coal taken from the altar with a pair of tongs. The seraph touched Isaiah's mouth saying,

See, this has touched your lips;
Your iniquity is removed;
And your sin is wiped away.

Then the change occurred in the tightness of Isaiah's fear, hurt and pain. The hot coal lifted the woeful lostness and bridged the separation. The power of God's presence healed his painful awareness, it did not destroy or punish. The blinding awareness of his own hurt and unworthiness yielded to new sight of God's intention for him. Inwardly, we can almost feel the blazing conflict resolved into new life. God's presence called him into a new sense of himself, opening him to hear the call of God's query,

Whom shall I send;
Who shall go for me!

This dramatic experience is witness to the power of God's presence which heals the deep wounds and self-deception in our lives, yielding a new openness to life's graceful reality.

None of us are Isaiah, chosen as the special messenger to the people in the time of national crisis. However, the process that takes place in the confrontation of God's presence is true to life itself. It takes place in common ways as well as in the intense fashion as in Isaiah's life. This process is highlighted in the many reported experiences of the persons in the history of religion: Moses with the burning bush; Amos in the countryside; Paul on the Damascus road; the multitude of persons who experienced Jesus. The elements of the experience are common in the endless unreported witnesses through the ages. The healing and growth come from the deep inward struggle and stress when confronted with the presence of God. Some of you here may be in the midst of such a process now.

Let me explore with you the stages or steps by which it flows.

Such experiences with God's presence often start with some disrupting event—a loss, a disturbance, a death, a major change of life situation, a painful anxiety that will not go away. Life begins to feel separated from itself and confusion often sets in. These experiences can come from events over which we have no control. An accident, the loss of employment, the breakdown of a marital relationship, a death of a loved one or friend. On a national or global scale, such disruption may occur as in war, terrorism, radical shifts in the economy. In Isaiah's case, it was the death of the king that disrupted the stability of the nation.

The second step is the attempt to see our way through the disturbance, loss or confusion. At such times, we often go where we have found help before or to a place of comfort or security. Many turn to religious feelings and experience such as church or talking with the pastor. Others return to the place of relaxation and quiet, such as the ocean or mountains. Others turn to doctors, medicine, alcohol, drugs or interminable work. The effort is to find a place where we can see a vision of solution or pathway through the disturbance. Isaiah's practice was to go to the Temple. There he hoped to discover an answer to his confusion. In simple terms, we go to that place where we hope to find God.

Often the process stops here, oscillating between disturbance and seeking. Of course if we seek places where the promised help cannot be given, such as in alcohol, drugs, false religion, no movement takes place and we become more disturbed, distressed, and depressed. Such false gods only intensify the self-deception.

There are those moments, however, when the promised help does come—given as an act of Grace. The fullness of God's presence appears to us. How, why and where cannot be controlled and manipulated by our fervent longings and anxieties. There occurs in us the time of readiness and receptivity to God's presence. Our eyes are opened to see the reality of our situation and the profound Holiness within life itself.

When this occurs, we are overwhelmed by our own inadequacy and self-deception. Who we thought we were and how we have been attempting to handle the situation hits like a hammer on an anvil, as with Isaiah. Another often repeated witness to this comes from the experience of alcoholics, "I hit rock bottom." Those with terminal illness testify to that time when the reality of their impending death appears in undeniable force. Reality confronts—God's presence confronts—and in the face of it, we experience an overwhelming sense of separation, alienation, helplessness and inadequacy. It feels like the healing is worse than the disease.

At that moment, something moves—as with the seraph in the Holy of Holies. We are touched in some manner or fashion. In modern parlance, there is a "breakthrough." This may happen through another person who is present with us. It may happen through a sermon or prayer. It may happen through a strange series of events. The process moves toward healing and wholeness. In pastoral psychotherapy for instance, there are moments in the process where the person's life is filled with a sense of presence, a deep confrontation of an inner reality of that person's life and an awareness that some deep pain or hurt has been touched and begins to heal. This is the kind of moment about which Paul Tillich spoke in his sermon on acceptance.

> Sometimes at that moment a wave of light breaks into our darkness, and it is as though a voice were saying: "You are accepted. *You are accepted,* accepted by that which is greater than you, and the name of which you do not know. Do not ask for the name now; perhaps you will find it later. Do not try to do anything now; perhaps later you will do much. Do not seek for anything; do not perform anything; do not intend any-

thing. *Simply accept the fact that you are accepted!*" If that happens to us, we experience grace. After such an experience we may not be better than before, and we may not believe more than before. But everything is transformed. In that moment, grace conquers sin, and reconciliation bridges the gulf of estrangement. And nothing is demanded of this experience, no religious or moral or intellectual presupposition, nothing but *acceptance.*

The next stage or step in the process is the openness to once again begin to look outward. For Isaiah it was the inner capacity to hear God's voice: "Whom will I send? Who will go for me?" This was Isaiah's call into new life. Each of us has the unique movement of our self into new awareness and call to mission. For some, it is a change in relating to others, a change in career, a change in the way time and money are spent, a change in the priority values which guide and direct our lives.

The concluding result of such inward change is a significant growth in the deep and abiding trust in life itself—ourselves, others, God. Our sense of inward well-being is accepted and the threats, insecurities and anxieties from inside yield to trust and well-being. For Isaiah, he could trust the message which God gave him to tell the people, as ironic and confusing as it seemed. For Isaiah, he could trust his own and God's authority for it rang with truth and reality. The healing of God's presence is the movement toward deep and abiding trust.

The dynamic process in the healing presence thus, is: disturbance, going to a place for help, confrontation with the fullness of God's presence, woeful awareness of self-deception, a touch of God's grace which turns the pain to healing (a connectedness), an outward view of life and the inward awareness of deep and abiding trust.

I recently visited my aging parents, residents of a nursing home in a small northern Minnesota town. A friend who is a resident there, and who suffers from crippling arthritis and constant pain, related this experience. This friend, prone to pneumonia, had been hospitalized the previous week. The absence of her lively presence among the other residents stirred deep concern for her recovery, for she was very sick. Another resident, confined to a wheelchair because of a stroke, wanted to do something. With no opportunity nor money to purchase a "get well card," she made one with her unparalyzed hand. She visited all the other residents and staff, obtaining their signatures on the home-made card. For those unable to sign, she signed for them. She wheeled herself to the hospital, which is connected to the home, and visited Johnnie the arthritic. In presenting the card, she apologized for the home-made character of her work. Immediately, Johnnie saw the significance: "Don't apologize—you gave of yourself!"

In that setting, that is the healing touch, the burning coal, which mediates the presence of God in the midst of suffering. Doing is made real by the being and giving of self. How many times we have heard this in our religious education and how often we are still blind to those significant moments of the healing touch from those around us. O God, forgive our blindness.

Pastoral care and counseling have become formal words in the profession of ministry and the life of the church. At the core of our life together, care and counseling are the process of that healing touch through the Presence of God. Psychotherapy, often a formal and foreboding word, is a relationship in which the dynamic steps of moving from disruption and loss to deep abiding trust can take place. This indeed is the ministry we have in the care and counsel of each other.

The healing process is the very source of life itself. For Isaiah, it occurred in his dramatic moment in the Temple. The process by which the presence heals is highlighted in this transforming event in his life, but the healing presence is accessible in the daily round of everyday events. To perceive and accept the healing touch—the burning coal—is God's grace which transforms our hurt, fear and anxiety into inner health and wholeness. Sin and separation are transformed into salvation. Amen.

Philippians 2:5–11
Isaiah 25:1–4a

FROM STRENGTH TO STRENGTH

Theodore H. Runyon, Jr., D. Theol.

Ted Runyon is a professor of systematic theology who is sensitive to the total training of seminary students and the situations they are called to minister in.

His sermon *From Strength to Strength* was preached to graduating seniors at Candler School of Theology, Emory University, who would soon be taking pastoral charges at the end of the 1960's. In it he cautions us as pastors that Jesus did not call people into hurt and pain but out of it, did not call people to be simply children of God but mature sons and daughters of God. He develops the implication that we should avoid the common trap of ministering and preaching to people only at the point of their vulnerability and weakness, but should address ourselves also to their strengths. (On this subject see also William H. Willimon's *The Gospel for the Person Who Has Everything,* Judson Press, Valley Forge, 1978.)

Writing from his prison cell in Berlin-Tegel Military Prison, Dietrich Bonhoeffer commented to a friend that for most of its nineteen hundred year history, Christianity has taken the "religious" approach to humanity. The religious approach he defined as it is exemplified in the world's religions generally, where gods are understood in terms of their power, their might, their ability to do what people cannot do. Persons, on the other hand, are religious precisely insofar as they recognize their weakness, their finitude, their final impotence in the face of those powers which threaten their existence, the awareness characterized by Schleiermacher as the "feeling of absolute dependence," that helplessness in the face of the awesome powers of the universe experienced by ancient and modern people alike. Thus most basically persons qualify as religious if they have a genuine sense of their own weakness plus an awareness of a powerful God who transcends them and who can save them in their extremity. In the Scripture passage that we read this morning Isaiah says, "Strong peoples will glorify thee, O Lord." Yet our preaching, our apologetics, our whole approach to the conversion process, have been geared to appeal to persons at the point of their weakness, that is, to appeal to their sense of loneliness, lostness, fear, anxiety, guilt, despair. Only when they become aware of their own utter bankruptcy can they properly appreciate the saving power of God; only then will they be in the proper frame of mind to be open to grace streaming down from a sovereign Lord, mercy bestowed by a righteous Judge.

What happens to this approach, however, when applied to contemporary people, asks Bonhoeffer, that is, to people for whom it is no longer as obvious as it was to their ancient forebears that they are essentially powerless, the hopeless victim of forces in their world over which they have no control? What happens when this approach confronts the persons who are not especially unhappy, not in any great pain, not in imminent danger of death, in other words, persons who do not understand themselves to be caught up in existential Angst, living at the outer limits of their resources? How do we approach them? And you have plenty of people just like this whom you know in the charge you serve on weekends; and they'll be there in the church to which you will be assigned when you graduate from Candler. What do you do with these people?

Let's face it. They're the ones who frustrate us the most. The weak ones we know how to deal with. We can get on their wave length in a hurry. All it takes is a touching sermon and a notice in the bulletin that the pastor is available in his/her office for counseling Monday, Wednesday, and Friday afternoons, from 2–5, and people will come. They'll come and spill out their problems and fears and frustrations, and if you're a good listener and inspire confidence they'll be back for another session next week. These are the people we appreciate because they enable us to operate in the role in which we see ourselves: helping people in their needs. They are the people to whom we preach, to whose situation we can speak indirectly—though in veiled fashion, of course, so that any resemblance to persons living or dead will be purely coincidental. They give us a sense that we are fulfilling our calling. That is, they meet us on the grounds where they are weak but we are strong. They come to us when we're either in the chair of the pastoral counselor or in the pulpit of the preacher. They are in the position of the client, the patient. They need something; we've got it to give.

But what about the majority which does not feel the need for our product most of the time? The majority who may get into occasional scrapes and jams, but usually feel pretty independent and self-sufficient. Are they the stiffnecked generation of which the Bible speaks? What do we do with the person who, as Bonhoeffer says, "won't see his happiness is really damnation, his health sickness, his vigor and vitality despair; if he won't call them what they really are, the preacher is at his wit's end. Such a man must be a hardened sinner of a particularly pernicious type"? (Letter of June 30, 1944, *Letters and Papers from Prison.*) Must our ministry be geared to people's needs in their moments of weakness at the edge of their existence, or can we reach them at the center of their lives where they ordinarily live, indeed at the points where they feel most competent and most strong? Is there a gospel for the strong persons in their non-religious life as well as for the weak persons in their feelings of religious dependence?

Bonhoeffer claims there is, that indeed Jesus himself did not call people into a sense of sin, shame and guilt, but out of it! He did not call them into sickness and weakness as a condition of hearing his gospel, but healed the sick and did not question the value of health and happiness as such. He was not an ascetic, as John the Baptist was, and he was obviously not religious enough according to the standards of the Judaism of his day. Yet he had a gospel, a gospel which could be heard by all. He called for "repentance," to be sure, but what was that repentance, the *metanoia,* that *turning around* for which he called?

Here Bonhoeffer turns the tables on us again. What are we called to? To join God in his suffering—that's right, in his suffering, to join him at the point where he is risking himself for people. The strong person is called to join the "weak" God. "That is *metanoia,*" he says, "and that is what makes a man and a Christian" (July 21, 1944).

Now that's really offensive! Bad enough that Bonhoeffer should question the traditional religious picture of the weak person. Of what possible good, however, is a weak God? Yet from Jesus we hear, "Could ye not watch with me one hour?" And Bonhoeffer comments, "It is not by his omnipotence that Christ helps us but by his weakness and suffering" (July 16, 1944). What can this mean?

Let's illustrate this first in terms of the life of the *pastor*. One of our STD students, Mr. James Buskirk, told me of an approach he has used in Mississippi which I commend to you. He sets aside half a day each week to be with his laypeople in *their* job, the place where they normally operate. That is, he doesn't demand that they come to him, or even meet him halfway—on the golf course. But he goes to the place where they are strong and he is weak, where they are knowledgeable and he is a mere layman, where they feel competent and secure and he feels a little uneasy. In the process he has discovered why the laypeople feel uneasy relating to the preacher on the preacher's strong ground. And he has also discovered that it is possible to be pastor to a person at the point of their strength, in their profession, on their job, or on their farm. But there his pastoring does not need to take the form of religious language. In fact, he refuses to be drawn into pious conversation until the point is reached where it is possible for the laypersons to talk in a down-to-earth and ordinary way about how they carry out their stewardship and their Christian commitment through their job.

This is ministry to the strong persons at the point of their strength, but it is possible only if the pastor is willing to risk weakness, only if, like God, he or she can be there at the point where people are strong without needing to dominate or reduce them, but calling them to exercise their strength responsibly in the world.

Perhaps another illustration can make even clearer what is involved. Last week it came to light that the helicopter pilot whose complaint touched off the investigation of the alleged massacre at My Lai was Hugh C. Thompson, Jr. of Decatur, Georgia. His parents live over on Nelson Ferry Road, off Scott Boulevard, about two miles from the Emory campus. Young Thompson is obviously a man of considerable moral stamina, for he not only lodged the complaint which since has made him the object of attack by right-wing extremists as betraying his country and undermining the morale of his fellow servicemen, but on the day of the incident itself, "he spotted fifteen young children trying to hide in a bunker, (landed his helicopter) and evacuated them to a secure area. Moments later he located a wounded Vietnamese child and, disregarding his own safety, he again landed and evacuated the child" (*Atlanta Constitution,* Friday, November 28, 1969, page 8-A). Another account said that "as he picked up (that) child he was faced by a rifle-brandishing officer who told him to leave the child and go. (Thompson called to) his machine gunner to train his sights on the officer and proceeded to evacuate the child anyway" (*Atlanta Constitution,* Sunday, November 20). He then radioed headquarters and got the order sent back to the ground forces to stop the shooting, saving the lives of the approximately one hundred and fifty civilians who had not yet been killed.

Curious about the background of a man with that kind of courage and conviction, I talked with his father, Hugh Thompson, Sr., about his son. "What kind of religious background did he have?" "Nothing special; he grew up going to the Episcopal Church in Stone Mountain." "Was he especially religious?" "No, not really. I mean he was a normal boy, interested in Scouts and then in football. We raised him to make his own decisions. We didn't try to hold on to him. We felt we could trust him. He had enough of the mind of Christ in him, you know, that we trusted him." Mr. Thompson seemed a little embarrassed that he had put it just that way, but my thoughts went to the passage in Philippians, and then I understood what he was saying,

> Have this mind in you, which was in Christ Jesus, who, though he was in the form of God, did not count equality with God a thing to be grasped, but emptied himself, taking the form of a servant . . . (2:5–7).

I don't know whether Mr. Thompson meant to say all that, but it helps to explain his son. Here is a strong man, not especially religious, but yet who risks his life where the need of persons calls him to disregard his own safety, to come down and join them in their suffering and danger in order to minister to them and release them. Like God, the strong person can risk being weak. Not preoccupied with themselves and their own salvation they can afford to venture out when the need of others calls, even where there is danger of losing themselves.

So as you go to minister to your people, be aware of the Hugh Thompsons and potential Hugh Thompsons who are there, those who are not especially religious, who operate out of strength rather than weakness, but who, touched by the mind of Christ, at the right moment, the moment which calls for responsible action, are able to risk their strength in compassion and service. For "that is *metanoia,* and that is what makes a Christian and a human."

Prayer: "Strong peoples will glorify thee, O Lord." Make us true ministers of thy gospel to persons at the point of their strength. Amen.

STUMBLING TO THE TRUTH

1 Corinthians 1:19–24
Exodus 3:1–12

Nancy E. Donny

> *Nancy Donny is a United Church of Christ minister who has a background in Clinical Pastoral Education as well as experience with pastoral counseling. Her particular focus of pastoral concern and expertise is in designing liturgy that encourages participation of all congregants from young children to the elderly. She is presently on the staff of South Congregational Church in East Hartford, Connecticut.*
>
> Her sermon *Stumbling to the Truth* is a wonderful example of how one with a personally prolific vocabulary and vast range of reading can use the simplest language and employ a basic story telling technique to communicate effectively with a wide variety of people in a single congregation. She uses the story of her own experience growing up with "radio preachers" as a way of expounding the themes of wisdom, mystery, and humility found in 1 Corinthians.

I grew up in a house peopled by preachers. I don't mean to say that my father or mother were ministers, or that they preached to us kids, though they did sometimes do that, on subjects other than the Bible! The preachers to whom I am referring were not members of my family. In fact, they were utter strangers, mysterious people whose faces I never even saw. They were, as you may have guessed by now, radio preachers.

My father loved those radio preachers, and he listened to them every evening and on the weekends. We kids, naturally, did not think it was cool to listen to radio preaching, or any other kind for that matter. I don't recall ever sitting down on purpose in front of the radio to listen to a sermon. But it was hard to escape them entirely. The preaching pervaded our entire home atmosphere. Scraping carrots in the kitchen, I would hear Garner Ted Armstrong's emphatic admonitions about the lost tribes of Israel, who, he solemnly assured us, had taken up residence in the U.S. and Great Britain. Doing homework in my room I would be distracted by Billy Graham's unmistakable rhythms floating up from the room below. Even down in our basement, roller skating or playing orphans-marooned-on-a-desert-island, we could not escape the preaching. The disembodied tones of the New York Presbyterian or the man from the Lutheran Hour would always come sneaking down the heating shaft, frequently ruining the mood of our games entirely.

I learned a lot from those men, and they were all men, of the radio ministry. For one thing, I learned that there was no such thing as "the" Bible, no such thing as "the" Word of God; I sometimes wondered whether, indeed, there was such a thing as "one" God. Every radio preacher I heard quoted the Bible, but somehow their messages didn't always jibe with one another. I heard that the Bible teaches us to serve and love each other. I heard that the Bible has a secret formula for success in this life. The Bible supported the war in Vietnam; the Bible was totally against all war. The Bible upheld the American way of life; the Bible hated all riches and luxury. On and on went the different versions of "the" Bible which the radio preachers preached. And their versions of God were equally varied.

One man suggested that God was a suffering servant. Another proclaimed the angry and jealous God sometimes found in the Old Testament as the "real" God. God was a kind old man with a paternal outlook. God was a ferocious judge separating lambs from goats and dooming the latter to eternal fire and brimstone. God was the peacemaker. God was the one who divided us from even our own family.

It was hard for me to get all these Bibles and Gods together. I wondered which preacher, if any, was right. But, being a child, I didn't worry about it for long; I simply asked my Dad which preachers were closest to the truth, and accepted what he told me.

Looking back now, the radio preachers remind me, in a way, of the Jews and Greeks whom Paul mentions in the passage we heard today. The Jews, he says, demand signs, and the Greeks seek wisdom. That is, when searching for the true God, the Jews looked for signs of God's power—actions in history—which demonstrated to them very clearly that God was God. This emphasis on signs was a part of the Jews' very being, their nature, their understanding of who they were. God had, from the beginning, revealed Himself to them in signs which showed caring for and involvement with them in a saving way. God brought the Jews out of bondage. God fed them manna in the wilderness, and brought them to the Promised Land. God gave them the Ten Commandments, God parted the sea of reeds, God led them to victory in battles. The Jews understood God as one who acted, who did powerful deeds, in their daily lives, in history. So, Paul says, the Jews demand signs. And some of my radio preachers were like these Jews. In every event, they looked for a sign of God, usually of the coming of the Kingdom on earth. World catastrophes such as famine or earthquake were always linked to some passage in Revelation which showed that the end of time was near. The taking away of prayer in the schools was another portent. One person even said that he had been noticing more white horses on farms than ever before, and that this was a sign of the coming of God. They looked for, and found, signs of God's actions all about them.

Many of the other radio preachers were like the Greeks Paul mentions. The Greeks sought God through wisdom. The Greeks became famous for their love of knowledge and wisdom. Their method of seeking it, philosophy, has come down to us today as rational enquiry. The highest form of this, for us, is embodied in the scientific method. We work from facts, empirical evidence, back to the underlying principles behind them. Radio preachers using this method liked to give rational reasons for their beliefs. They applied scientific principles to the study of the Bible, and showed by deductive reasoning the correct interpretations of each passage, and, thereby, the correct, the true, God.

I have a feeling that most of us fall into the category of either Greeks or Jews. We either search for God through signs, miracles of power in our lives, or we look for rational proofs of God's existence, and rational reasons for everything God does. Yet Paul, in the First Letter to the Corinthians, notes that this is a mistake. The main thing wrong with trying to find God through wisdom, as in the scientific method, or through signs of God's great power, as manifested in winning battles, returning prayer to the schools, or whatever, is that in doing so we run the grave danger of making our own wishes into gods and worshiping them, instead of the one true God. This is not to say that God does not act in history, or that God is not present in scientific enquiry. But it is to say, as Paul warns, that we are not likely to find God in places which seem obvious to us. The Jews looked for God as a mighty miracle worker. The Greeks tried to find God by philosophical reflection. But God came in a way which was unlooked-for by either group, namely in the person of Jesus the Christ, and him crucified.

Paul says that Christ crucified was a "stumbling block" to both Jews and Greeks, and I would imagine that this is putting it very mildly. To the Jews, a Savior who got himself crucified without even trying to raise armies or call down angels to save him must have been no Savior at all. And to the Greeks, the very idea of God having a human body was just as bad as God being crucified. Yet, Paul says, to those who are called, both Jews and Greeks, Christ is the power of God and the wisdom of God—both the things the Greeks and Jews were looking for, but found in an unexpected place.

But how does this translate to us? We aren't really surprised to find God revealing Himself through Jesus' death and resurrection; after all, we've heard about it all our lives. Perhaps, because it seems so familiar, we miss the radical message of the crucifixion. This message seems to be, as Paul hints, that God is revealed to us in the place and way we least likely expect. For the Greeks and Jews this was definitely true, and it might be for us, too. The Bible cites many instances of this kind of thing. In the first passage we read today, God was revealed to Moses, who was very surprised to be chosen as an instrument of the Lord. The burning bush which was not consumed was probably the last thing Moses had ever expected to see, and to find God through such a thing must have been a shock. Similarly, in the New Testament, John tells the story of Jesus and the woman at the well. This woman, who had been married five times and was apparently an adulteress, seemed an unlikely person for Jesus to be passing the time of day with. But Jesus not only did that, he chose her as the first person to whom he revealed his true nature as the Son of God.

Maybe we forget strange little stories like these until something similar happens to us. I think some of those radio preachers did. They were so busy looking for a God who was like them they often overlooked the real God. By picking and choosing aspects of God which appealed to them, and preaching those aspects only, they avoided having to wrestle with God in God's reality, which is always something other than what we are. If I am a Greek, interested in spiritual life and mind over matter, chances are that God is going to sneak up on me as a regular old human being. If I am a Jew, looking for God to be revealed with armies and thunder and lightning, God will probably show up as a weak, suffering person. If I am a rational young minister, looking for God in the pages of some heavy theologian, it's a good bet that I might better be looking in that hospital ward I'm avoiding visiting, or talking with that parishioner who seems so stuck-up and aloof. No matter who I am, God is probably waiting for me right now in the very place or thing or person which I avoid most. For the foolishness of God is wiser than human, and the weakness of God is stronger, says Paul.

Probably the most way-out person who has ever called himself a radio preacher is Reverend Ike. He is a great manipulator, both of his listeners, and of the Bible. "Do you want pie in the sky when you die?" he asks. "Or would you rather have a million dollars and a big pink Cadillac right now?" Then he tells you that by sending money you can receive his free book on how to get both, based entirely on Scripture. . . .

Few of us dare to be as openly manipulative as some preachers who are obviously show-biz persons in the "preaching" trade because of the money they finagle from people rather than because of any faith in God. Yet I wonder if we are not all a little bit like such people deep in our hearts. Don't we all manipulate God, or try to, when we look for the God we want to see? Isn't it a kind of Idolatry when we declare emphatically that God says this, or the Bible says that is right, and are telling only a part of what the Bible says? And especially when that part of the Bible is the part which most agrees with our views on life?

Some of those radio preachers I used to hear were Greeks seeking a rational God they could understand—and thereby control, manipulate. Others were Jews, looking for God in signs they could see—and control, manipulate. But the vast majority of radio preachers preached the same message of Jesus the Christ, and him crucified. We won't find God by the wisdom of the world, that is, our own wisdom, for it consists entirely in the desire to measure God by our own standards. But God's foolishness is wiser than our wisdom, and God's weakness is stronger than our strength. God will be God, no matter what we try to do to make things otherwise. And God will continue to be revealed to us in the hidden, the unexpected, the surprising—the crucified Christ. For this mystery of salvation, thanks be to God. Amen.

Predicaments

THE OBSTACLE OF DOUBLEMINDEDNESS

William E. Hulme, Ph.D.

William E. Hulme has been a steady contributor of books and articles to the field of pastoral care and counseling for many years. He is currently a Professor in the Department of Pastoral Theology and Ministry of Luther-Northwestern Seminaries in St. Paul, Minnesota.

The depth of his historical as well as contemporary knowledge of pastoral care plus his precise, economical use of words is reflected in his sermon *The Obstacle of Doublemindedness.* The doublemindedness that James writes of, or the ambivalence that modern counselors point to, is the subject of the sermon. Hulme succinctly outlines the predicament of ambivalence using contemporary and historical illustrations. He then presents a classical exposition of the dynamics of grace in relation to its healing. (Hulme has expanded his thought of doublemindedness into a full book published by Harper & Row in 1982 under the title *Dealing with Double-Mindedness.*)

In Book VIII of his *Confessions,* St. Augustine is bemused over what he calls a great mystery. The mind can tell the body what to do—such as, "raise your hand"—and up goes the hand. But the mind can tell the mind what to do—such as, "get at the assignment that is due tomorrow"—and nothing may happen. Is not the mind closer to itself than it is to the body? In fact, should not the very act of the mind's directing itself be the same as its carrying it out?

In reflecting on this mystery Augustine concluded that perhaps he has been under an illusion, namely, that he has *one* mind. What if there were *two* minds? Then the mystery would clear. For what the one mind has the other would lack, and what the one mind wanted the other would resist.

In a different setting Augustine gave an example of his own "two minds" over his sexual problems. His parody of prayer was, "Lord, make me chaste, but not yet."

1. *Doublemindedness in the Epistle of James*

Augustine was illustrating the *doublemindedness* described in the Epistle of James. A doubleminded person, says James, is like a wave of the sea that is driven and tossed by the wind—and therefore is unstable in all his or her ways. Such a person is unable to receive anything from the Lord. (James 1:6–8) The analogy of doublemindedness to a wave of the sea being driven and tossed by the wind corresponds to the clinical word, *ambivalence.* Ambivalence (ambi-valence) means literally both strengths, or two strengths in opposition. An ambivalent person is one who is driven and tossed by opposing forces within.

Our doublemindedness can trip us up at the most inopportune times. In my first year in the ministry I was asked by a college friend to officiate at her wedding. When I consented she stated that she and her fiancée would like to be married at a particular restaurant. Again I said *yes* but inwardly I resisted. I said *yes* because I wanted to please; I said *no* within because I prefer to solemnize marriages in the church sanctuary. But I went ahead with the plans. Even the rehearsal was held in the restaurant, as we made a makeshift altar out of a table and used a staircase as an aisle. I got through the rehearsal and even the wedding itself rather well until near the close when I said, "What God has put asunder, let no man join together!" Realizing immediately that I had reversed the verbs, I knew I had only a split second to decide whether or not to correct it. I took a quick look at the assembled people—and noting no sense of shock on their faces, I went on with the service. But I knew what had happened—my doublemindedness had tripped me up.

James is an early analyst, investigating the inner dynamics not only of doublemindedness but also of repression and self-deception. The word translated doubleminded is actually *two souled.* Goethe uses these words when he has Faust say, "Two souls, alas, dwell within my breast apart." The description is psychological of course, and not ontological.

A doubleminded person, says James, is unstable in all his or her ways. The word translated *unstable* means literally, *not according to one's being*. Being unstable, therefore, means not being in charge of oneself—being out of control. This condition is best described in the First Step of Alcoholics Anonymous: "Our lives have become unmanageable."

2. *The Miracle of Grace*

Because of its disintegrating effect I see doublemindedness as a major obstacle to change, in my pastoral counseling experience as well as in my experience with myself. It is a major obstacle to what St. Peter calls our growth in grace, or, in the words of St. Paul, a major way by which we quench the Spirit of God in our lives.

Doublemindedness throws light on our sinful nature. When we confess in our various worship forms that we are poor miserable sinners, the most common understanding of these words is that we are weak and impotent—so wretchedly and sinfully weak that mercy could be expected. But if we understand the words *poor miserable sinner* to mean defiant, strong, resister of God, the picture is different. Soren Kierkegaard said that the essence of sin from a Christian point of view is not in negation but in defiance. That is, sin is not essentially negating something but positioning something, not the absence of something, a weakness, but the possession of something—a taking of a position over against God. In our doublemindedness we are actually connivers in our own falls, conspirators in our defeats, enablers in our yielding to temptation, forgers of our own imprisoning chains. Lord, have mercy on me, a weak impotent sinner. Yes, why not? But mercy for a defiant resister, saboteur, hypocrite—this takes a miracle!

And this is the Good News! The miracle has happened—the miracle of grace! God is reconciled with me in my duplicity—in my doublemindedness.

This miraculous reconciliation provides the freedom to become singleminded—here and there, now and then. First of all we are able to *see* our doublemindedness. There is now no condemnation—even for our doublemindedness—for those who are reconciled to God through Christ. It is the fear of condemnation that moves one to repress—to evade—not to see the doublemind. There is a radical difference between being a doubleminded person and being a *forgiven* doubleminded person. The miracle of grace makes possible a widening of our awareness of who we are, and at the same time a widening of our awareness of who God has called us to be. Through forgiveness we have a growing, expanding consciousness.

Like a prophet out of the Old Testament James says, "Purify your hearts, you men of double mind." (James 4:8) Kierkegaard said, "Purity of heart is to will one thing." This is what happens— again and again—as we are enabled by the Spirit to *affirm*, in the midst of our doublemindedness, our identity in Christ.

"BE ANGRY BUT DO NOT SIN" (Eph 4:26)

Ephesians 4:22–29
Romans 14:1–19

Gregory J. Johanson

Greg Johanson is a United Methodist Minister who has brought to ten years of parish experience a special training and interest in Clinical Pastoral Education and Pastoral Counseling. Recently he served as Chaplain and Director of Counseling Services at the Plaza Santa Maria Hospital, Ltd. in Baja, California. He presently lives with his wife Hope and son Leif in the Chiloquin-Beatty area of Southern Oregon. There he serves in ministry with Native American and rural populations while continuing doctoral studies in clinical psychology.

In *Be Angry But Do Not Sin,* Johanson deals specifically with the issue of anger though the gist of the sermon could be applied to many emotions as well; "be sad, but do not sin," "be jealous but do not sin," etc. It was delivered to his local congregation in Oregon in the normal course of preaching through the lectionary.

From a pastoral perspective it seems to me that one of the issues we deal with as members of the church is simply what to make of ourselves; how to make sense out of or integrate all the various feelings and moods we experience within a Christian frame of reference and meaning. One of the most troublesome and burdensome emotions we grapple with in particular is our anger. I think it is fair to say that a great number of us, including myself, were originally drawn to the church or to God because we thought we might find a sanctuary of peace where our angers, fears, and pains would somehow be transcended or banished. And some of us have worked very hard to make this the case. We have said or felt that anger was out of place in the life of a Christian or of a church. But when it inevitably worked its way to the fore, we have been thrown into a crisis where we doubted either our own discipleship or the reality of faith. All this is to say that I think the subject is a live issue for many of us, though I'm aware that we all experience it in different ways. I would like us to consider it this morning, then, by looking especially to Paul's words of guidance to the church at Ephesus, "Be angry but do not sin."

To begin with, **Be Angry.** Why?

1. Because anger is a part of our being. God made us this way. This is a simple affirmation of God as the Creator of the world, and an affirmation that His creation is good (Gen 1:31). We know we are angry people; we experience anger. We know God made us and we assume and trust as naive Christians that it was for some good purpose. The only other option is to tempt ourselves, as Jesus was tempted, to believe that the demonic is in control of the world, that there is an evil co-creator alongside God who creates "not good" things. This would be heresy. We affirm God as the *one* God and Creator of us all. There is no other beside Him evil or otherwise.

So Paul is saying in effect: *you are* children of God created in His image, so be who you are. Be angry; that is part of you. Don't try to be someone you are not. That would be both pretentious and impossible. It has taken me a long time to realize the truth of this. I have fought it because most of the anger I remember seeing as I grew up was destructive, and it scared me, and I determined to get away from it. But I can't do it. I cannot deny or run from some part of who I am as a child of God. It is always there. I cannot change myself into someone I am not. I cannot play God. He has created me in a certain way, and I am helpless to change it. You or I, neither one of us can control our feelings. They are a given. Sad things we experience touch our sadness. Funny things we encounter make us feel like laughing. Joyous things infect us and bring out our joy, whether we had determined to be a grouch all day or not. And angry things touch our anger. We are built that way. It is part of our creation.

The question then is never to be or not to be angry. That is a given. And the problem is not how to get rid of the anger because that is an impossibility (except for surgically removing it as in "One Flew Over the Cuckoo's Nest"). Basically our faith sets us free to be angry and not fight to keep from experiencing it. Once we accept this, we can move on to the task of trying to search out the *wisdom* in its creation and see what we will do with it, which leads us to point two.

2. Be angry, let yourself experience your anger, because the more free we are to acknowledge our feelings, the more free we are to choose wisely what to do with them, how to use them. This really says two things.

A. It says that while we have no control over our feelings being touched or activated, we have every responsibility to exert control over what we do with our feelings. Feelings are never bad or good in themselves, they are just feelings. Nothing is clean or unclean in itself as Paul says in Romans. But like everything else in life we realize that they can be used for constructive or destructive ends, aims, ambitions, purposes, etc. So, while it is not our task to engage in a futile attempt to deny our God-given humanity, it is our task to take responsibility for deciding how we will use, express, and channel our humanity to be good stewards.

B. Then secondly it is good to realize that we do have a number of options for dealing wisely with feelings such as anger. Once we are aware of it, and it is in our consciousness, we can choose in many respects the time, place, person, or group in which our anger might best be used by being concealed, by being acknowledged or communicated directly, by being exhibited or acted out physically (driving out the money changers), or by being channeled into motivation for some task.

It might seem obvious to say that we can do more than one thing with our emotions for good or ill, but there are many of us who have the deep-seated belief that if we feel any anger toward our parents, children, or friends, that is the equivalent of doing them in, or rejecting them out of hand, or being separated from them. This is not true. Feelings are not the same as actions. Feelings can build a bond as well as a wall between people. And it is good to know that we have the opportunity and options for choosing wisely what we do with our feelings once we are aware of them, so that separation and loneliness do not have to be the inevitable result.

3. Now point three of why be angry is that if we do not acknowledge our anger and choose to do something wise with it, it will choose to do something with us. We can repress it, deny it,

project it, rationalize it, but it will not be denied. It will set up a barrier or block that will not allow for love or anything else until it is ministered to. Bruce Larsen gives us a good and somewhat humorous example of this in his book, *Ask Me to Dance.*

He says that he and his wife were at a conference getting dressed one morning. His wife was in the other room and so he turned on the TV. The only thing on was cartoons, but he watched them because he likes them. Pretty soon his wife Hazel said, "Do you have to watch cartoons?" And Bruce replied, "Well, there is nothing else on; besides what's wrong with cartoons?" So his wife then began to tell him what was wrong with them and he began to defend them and tell her what was right about them, and they were off to the races on a real creative cozy morning—until, however, they realized that what was going on had nothing to do with cartoons. They were really carrying over some anger and hurt from an incident the previous night which had seemed too painful to talk about then. The denied anger was coming out in a sidewise hostility over the unreal issue of the TV. The point to note is that anger would not be denied. It controlled them until they faced it and acknowledged it and worked through it. They were not free to love until they were free to be angry and hurt and talk with each other on a genuine level.

4. This is a fourth and concluding reason for why be angry. Because if we cannot be angry we cannot love. Putting a damper on one part of our soul inevitably puts a damper on other parts as well. We are able to love in proportion to our ability to feel in general, and to experience and express our anger in particular. Putting a great concrete lid on negative feelings, as we call them, puts the same lid on positive passions.

There are innumerable examples in counseling of strong silent type fathers trying to do a good job with their families, who have realized they were not really able to say or show the affection they might want and were consequently cheating themselves and their families. Getting into a little history with them oftentimes turns up the fact that their own fathers or people close to them were distant sorts of people, severe in some respects, or perhaps contemptuous of emotional natures. One man specifically recalled thinking in the midst of being unfairly beaten by his father, "He'll never get to me." And he was successful to an extent. He cut his father off as a person, by cutting off his power to affect him and make him angry. But then he ran into the problem later on of not being able to express adequately his love for his wife and children because he was also unable to be angry with them. He was however able to be nurtured back to health and wholeness through the ministry of a warm accepting group which affirmed both his anger and strength as well as his tenderness and care.

I would like to add at this point that the pastors and Christian people and non-Christian people who have been the most inspirational to me in my life have been the ones with the most complete souls—the ones who could be incensed with anger and rage like a prophet at some wrong, who could feel in their bones the grief of bereaved people and their sorrow, and who could be tickled inside out by the joy of a child or the foolishness of a peer. They have been the beautiful people.

To summarize: Be angry because God made us that way and because there is beauty and wisdom in being a whole person, grown up into the image of Christ.

But Do Not Sin.

Sinning, as opposed to being at one or at peace with our humanity, has to do with running from our humanity. It has more to do with becoming *separated* from ourselves and our fellow human beings, and God.

I get into sin, not when I say I'm angry, but when I go beyond this or away from it, and say damning and rejecting things about the other as a person. I can speak the truth in love and say that I personally am very angry when you do such and such. But if I start to say you are not as good a person as I am, you are not as worthy as I am, that I reject you as a person and as a Christian, as a member of my family or community, that I disdain, scorn, despise you and will attempt to disgrace, disregard, and disown you—then I am giving into my fear and am introducing a separation into the relationship. I am sinning.

You can sense how cold and chilling this begins to sound. It is no longer anger. It is more what I call hostility. Hostility implies distance, lack of respect, fear, and a rejection of the other as a person. Paul says while it is okay to be angry, don't sin, don't get caught up in what we have just termed hostility. Why?

1. Because of common sense. The church in Rome had its problems as we saw in Romans 14. There were both Jews and Gentiles in the church and some had declared independence from the Jewish law and some had not. Now this could simply be an angry affair with genuine differences of opinion. But it was more than this. Unfair things were being said. Name calling had started, one group calling the other "Libertines," and hearing the rejoinder of "Legalists."

Paul attempted to introduce a note of common sense into the affair. (1) He said remember neither one of you is in a good position to judge because we are all going to be found wanting under the ultimate judgment of God. This is similar to Jesus' point when he said do not think of yourself as superior to one who commits adultery when you have the same lust in your own heart. We are all in this together, and we are all working with the same basic God-given equipment. (2) And Paul goes on. Even if you are intellectually or academically right and know that no food is unclean in itself, don't cause harm and distress to a brother or sister by inciting them through eating things in front of them that throw them into a crisis of doubt and despair. (3) And in a similar vein, Paul says to the church at Corinth that we are all part of one body. It is not common sense for a leg, or hand, or eye, or ear, no matter how good it is, to say or think it can get along without the other parts, that it can exist in separation from any other part or the whole.

2. Paul always goes beyond the common sense reasons for not doing something. He adds: do not sin just because of the logic of not doing it; that probably won't be able to stop you anyway. Don't sin because of the person of Christ. In Romans 14 Paul says: look at Christ; look at the example we have in him.

A minister whose name I don't know points out that it takes more than common sense to lift us out of our pettiness and sin to other ground, it takes a person. He illustrates this with the time he was at a meeting with other ministers led by William Temple, Archbishop of York. He said there had been some heated controversy at dinner over the divorce canon, over the coming second world war and the issue of being a pacifist or militarist. The conversation was not pleasant, respectful, or flattering to anyone concerned. Then after dinner in the sitting room, the ministers probed the Archbishop for his position. And the report was that (1) he did not try to minimize any differences, that (2) he had his own convictions on which he stood firm, and that (3) one could not be small, petty, or cutthroat in his presence. He lifted the whole discussion up into another realm where honest differences still existed but a different spirit prevailed. People went away still disagreeing but with an entirely different attitude toward their opponents. Hopefully, this is the kind of power that can be generated by our trying to get in touch with the spirit of Christ—how it worked in him and can work in us.

3. There is a final even more powerful reason for us not to sin according to Paul. Don't sin because we now know through the coming of Christ that we are justified by grace. Or to put it another way, don't sin because the good news is that we don't need to anymore.

This kind of reasoning basically assumes that we only go beyond our anger to our hostility when we are fearful; when we have deep feelings of self-doubt that makes us wonder if we really are worthwhile, acceptable, lovable, etc. So in our fear and doubt we pin our claim to goodness on things outside ourselves—our accomplishments, our keeping the law, our being associated with the right political party, right race, church, etc. Then when someone challenges these allegiances we feel personally challenged and attacked, and in our fear we sin by retaliating with hostility. The more fearful and doubtful we are, the stronger and more vicious our counterattack.

The corresponding cure for sin in this context is for us to somehow get the message that we are justified by grace; that God through Christ and the church is trying to communicate that we are acceptable in our most basic givenness; that we can be secure in the knowledge of the love of God in Christ. With this security and knowledge we can then quit trying to prove anything to ourselves, quit putting our trust in externals. We can have definite opinions, get angry when they are trampled on but still be open to dialogue with others. We can even be in a position to change our position because we won't be standing on it for support. Our strength would be "in the Lord," in the good news. We will not have the need to sin because we will have been given that which we need and want already. We are all aware that it is the biggest persons who can afford to admit they are wrong, the one with the most reason to be prideful who can afford to be humble. The sure knowledge that we are loved and considered worthwhile gives us a sure foundation and the strength to risk, grow, be vulnerable, and hang in there through tough times, not opting for the way out of separating from ourselves those who disagree with us and get into conflict with us.

In Conclusion: Let's switch gears for the moment and say, this all sounds fine and good, "be angry but do not sin." But let's ask what if we do?

What if we do sin and can't pull off all that we have talked of? We can basically guarantee that we won't be able to pull it off in many respects. Our fears go deep, and we don't claim perfection in this life, only to be on a pilgrimage. What if we do sin? Well, again, that is what the gospel is all about. That is the good news. John says in his first letter:

> My children, I am writing this to you so that you may not sin; but if any one does sin, we have an advocate with the Father, Jesus Christ; and he is the expiation for our sins, and not for ours only but also for the sins of the *whole world*. (I John 2:1–3, 15–17)

We can always reflect, see our brokenness, make our confessions, realize again the affirmation of the Divine YES, get whatever help we need in attempting to responsibly move in a more redemptive direction, and find peace and strength in the grace of God. And for this, we can give thanks. Amen.

MALE AND FEMALE
Robert R. Ball, S.T.D.

Studies in pastoral psychology and experience with personal growth have been an integrative focus of the pastoral ministry of Robert R. Ball. He is currently pastor of Fremont Presbyterian Church in Sacramento, California. He published his first book, The "I Feel" Formula *in 1977 (Word Books). His sermon published here comes out of the local church context and reflects his interest in helping people find authentic, realistic ways of being through which to incarnate the Gospel.*

Male and Female explores the issue of sexuality. Ball creatively deals with it as a reality in life, as a particularly sensitive and expressive means of communcation between two human beings, and as a wondrous means of being exposed, known, and accepted within the grace of a mature marriage.

> The Lord God said, "It is not good that the man should be alone; I will make him a helper fit for him." (Genesis 2:18)

Even in this uninhibited age of ours, sex is still a terrifying subject. The statistics are that sexual problems are the leading cause of divorce in America, and the major area of conflict even in the marriages that manage to hang together. Most parents find it to be the most difficult of subjects to discuss with their children. Sex is so explosive that it is considered bad manners to talk about it in polite society; and even though it is discussed often and extensively elsewhere, it is usually done with a smirk and a smile—all of which is a back-handed tribute to the significant, sensitive place it occupies in our lives.

Nearly everyone tries to play down sex. The "purists" try to squelch it by never mentioning it, and by viewing those who do with a shocked indignation for being so coarse and crude. The "libertines" try to deny the importance of sex by treating it as if it were nothing but a simple, biological urge, something like eating your lunch. These opposing groups actually have a lot in common. Both are scared to death of this explosive charge within them, and they don't really know what to do with it.

What a contrast this is to the biblical approach. The only difference between human beings which the creation story thought to be important enough to mention is that God created only two kinds: boy human beings and girl human beings. Perhaps the Bible has something to say to us who are so hung-up on sex that it is the only way we have of classifying our movies.

I

In the first place, the Bible wants us to get it straight: We *are* sexual creatures. That's how God made us. Sex is a fundamental part of who we really are.

Our age has been characterized as one undergoing an "identity crisis." All of us are trying to discover "Who am I?" We want to know how we're doing as business men and women and as houseparents and as students and as well adjusted persons; but before we are ever any of these things, we are either male or female. That's who we are. As a result, one of the most critical questions going inside of all of us is, "How am I doing as a man, or as a woman?"

That's the question that the woman is asking when she wears a low-cut gown to a party. She hopes that the reactions she gets from the males will confirm to her that as a woman she's doing O.K. But if she isn't completely honest with herself that this is the question she's asking, when some man makes it too obvious that he has noticed what she wanted him to notice, she feels that she must act as if she were humiliated and infuriated by his vulgarity. Actually, the man only wanted her to notice that he was an alive and virile male, hoping to be assured that he was doing O.K. as a man. Being president of a big company has its rewards, but having a thick carpet and five telephones doesn't satisfy the deeper need to know that a man is appreciated for who he really is. *A significant part of who he really is, is a sexual being.* He needs to know, "How am I doing as a man?"

There are two basic ways of copping out on the fact that God has created us to be sexual beings, and both ways are equally as destructive to our real humanity. One way tells us that we should develop our personalities apart from sex, concentrating our attention on the "higher" things in life. The young bride who has been taught to regard sex as a base, animal impulse will have a pretty difficult time adjusting to the wild beast she marries. The other cop-out tells us to develop our sex life apart from the rest of our personality which makes of sex an amusing game to play when we get bored. To treat so meaninglessly something that is so fundamentally a part of all that we are ends up by making our whole lives look silly and meaningless. *The Bible says it very clearly: God has created us to be either male or female human beings. We can never be whole human beings until we have accepted and come to terms with the fact of our sexuality.*

II

In the second place, the Bible says that the reason God created the two sexes is that a person by himself or herself is incomplete and unfulfilled. We can never be whole, human beings unto ourselves. We cannot be who we are without other people.

God saw that man was lonely, so he filled the world around with a vast array of dazzling delights. You get the feeling that the writer of this story was looking right at us when he wrote it. When we get discouraged and exhausted in our efforts to establish satisfying relationships with other people, we very often look around us and say, "It's silly for me to be lonely. Look at all this great big beautiful world filled with fascinating things for me to study and do."

So we get ourselves occupied with football and motorcycles, business and science, ballet and gardening, bridge and tennis, livestock and hunting, and sometimes we even get ourselves all wrapped up in religion. But no matter how much effort we put into any of these endeavors, as worthwhile as they very well may be in themselves, none of them are able to answer our aching loneliness.

It was when Adam recognized that nothing else in all the world could make him feel wanted and necessary and appreciated that God created a woman for him. God has given us things of the world to *use* and people to *love*. When we turn that around, *loving things and using people,* then all of life goes out of whack. A man needs to know that he is appreciated and valued as a man by other men—but in a unique way by women. They are necessary to complete his male humanity. A woman needs to know that she is appreciated as a woman by other women—but in a unique way by men. They are necessary to complete her female humanity. Sex has been given to us as a means of communication for these and other important matters.

Because sex can be regarded as the most sensitive and expressive means of communication that exists between two human beings, I have found it helpful in examining "sex problems" to ask: Where has the communication broken down? I ask the people involved to look at what they have to say to each other, that is, at how they really feel about themselves and the other person. Whatever they happen to be feeling, that's what gets communicated through their sexual relationship.

If there is resentment, that comes through. If there is weak-kneed fear, it is felt. If there is a desperate, clinging, suffocating yearning for assurance, the other person feels buried beneath all those needs. The solution to these problems, it seems to me, is not to be found in better sex techniques but in looking at and working on how we feel about ourselves and what we have to say to each other.

As I talk to kids about their sexual fears and frustrations, I frequently discover that their problems arise from trying to say more through sex than they actually have to say. The problem, therefore, is inauthentic communication. This guy, let's say, wants so much to be assured that he is loved, that this chick thinks he's the greatest thing in the world, that she is so knocked in the head with him that there's no way she could hold anything back from him. So he tries to force, through sexual expression, a relationship between them which does not, in fact, exist. It may or may not seem deliriously wonderful at the moment, but that night when he gets home, he feels punk. He knows he was living out a lie.

But when the authenticity is there, sex is an irreplaceable way in which we are able to say to another person, "You are important. I like who you are. I care about you."

That is the word of life, the word without which we cannot live. It is the word which God sent into the world in Jesus Christ in human form, the word which we touch and taste in the Lord's Supper. Jesus said, "This is my *body* which is broken for you." A real relationship is one in which we are able to communicate who we really are to others, and able to receive their communication of themselves to us. The man who is confident and pleased about being a man allows the women with whom he communicates to be confident and pleased that they are women. The woman who is confident and pleased about being a woman allows the men with whom she communicates to be confident and pleased that they are men. God created the two sexes because a person by himself or herself is unfulfilled and incomplete.

III

The final verse in this passage tells us that the marriage relationship is a very special kind of thing, *the fullest relationship possible among human beings.*

> The man and his wife were both naked, and were not ashamed.

How many of us are willing for the naked truth about ourselves to be known? Who is willing to reveal how they hurt and what they hope in the depths of their being? It is a frightening prospect, being completely known; and that's why we spend a great deal of our time and effort trying to make sure that we will not be. We cover ourselves with cheerfulness or sullenness, with fine clothes or with rags, with education or ignorance, with religion or with unbelief—anything to keep from being exposed. *But sometimes, often by accident, when our guard is down, it happens that someone does see us and know us and approve of us.*

That glorious delight is how the lost sheep felt when he was found.

When someone knows us and accepts us and values us, we are no longer stuck with those frightening and inaccurate images we have of ourselves—the ones that make us ashamed, force us to cover up, and leave us feeling awkward and ill at ease in the presence of others. It's something like becoming a brand new person.

But there is no possiblity of our being fully known to everyone. We will dare to reveal our deepest selves only to a person in whom we have absolute trust and confidence that he or she will not make fun of us or run away from us. It takes a lot of time and effort, a lot of hurting and forgiving, to develop trust and commitment to each other in which that miracle can happen.

That's why the sex act itself cannot be shared frivolously or thoughtlessly. It is an honest communication only when two people are willing to make a continuing commitment to each other and to accept a continuing responsibility for each other.

> The man and his wife were both naked, and were not ashamed.

I have a minister friend back in Oklahoma who's been married for some thirty years now, a perfectly delightful person. One night he and I were driving back from a meeting in another city. He kept urging me to drive faster. I asked him why. When he told me, I said something like, "You old codger! You mean you're that excited to get home to your woman after all of these years?" He told me that they had never enjoyed each other so much ever before. They had been through a lot together and not all of it good. One time she actually left him. But through it all they had come to an honest, open, sharing kind of relationship that had him on fire to get home that night. I think that's what God intended sex to be.

The gospel of Jesus Christ says that we are accepted. That acceptance certainly includes our sexuality, for it is a basic ingredient of who we are. God isn't deceived in his acceptance. He knows that we have sometimes brought great pain to others and to ourselves—and that is very painful to him. But God doesn't destroy us when we are wrong. He forgives us in order that we might start anew, using our lives to be a blessing to others. Don't be afraid of yourself or your sexuality. God had good things in mind when he created you. God wants to use all that you are as a means of communicating his love to his people. *The most important decision a person ever makes is to accept God's acceptance. Then that person is able to accept himself or herself, to come alive as a real human being.*

The more men who are really men, with nothing to prove but love to give, and the more women who are really women, *with nothing to prove but love to give,* the more whole and human this world will be, *something like the Kingdom of God.*

WHO WOULD WANT TO SHOOT A POPE?

Bruce M. Hartung, Ph.D.

At the time he delivered "Who Would Want To Shoot a Pope?" Bruce M. Hartung preached on invitation from various Lutheran churches in the northern Illinois area as the then Director of the Pastoral Psychotherapy Institute in Park Ridge, Illinois. As of September 1, 1983 he became the new Executive Director of the Onondaga Pastoral Counseling Center, Syracuse, New York.

Who Would Want To Shoot a Pope? is a sermon that focuses on the traumatizing events that are part of our experience in the 1980's. Hartung deals in particular with the temptation this trauma brings to deaden ourselves with pessimism and withdrawal. In addition to bringing a biblical perspective to bear on the subject he illustrates the power of using a variety of particular, concrete examples to support and enliven generalizations in preaching.

In the *Chicago Tribune* accounts of the attempted assassination of Pope John Paul II, after the article which reported on the attempt itself, I was drawn immediately to a smaller article on one of the inside pages. It began as follows: "John Cardinal Cody, leader of Chicago's Catholic Archdiocese, said Wednesday that he sought to protect the Pope from surging crowds when he visited Chicago in October, 1979, but that Pope John Paul II said it wasn't necessary and responded, 'Who would want to shoot a Pope?'"

Now we know. Someone did. Mehmet Ali Agca did. Coming on the heels of the attempt on the life of President Reagan, one wonders what our world is coming to. With incidents of terrorism on the rise in the world, with people killing people daily in the United States, mostly with handguns, with Syria and Israel at missile point with each other, with the killing of three nuns and a laywoman in El Salvador, the world scene looks a mess. In the terror of our times, the question, "Who would want to shoot a Pope?" cannot be answered comfortably with "No one."

The response that I have heard from most people, besides the shock and dismay, is close to what I have just expressed. The thought is that our world and the people in it are worsening; that the world is becoming more and more violent; that we are less safe in our world; that evil seems to have the ascendancy over good. The assumption through this all is that times have changed. I do not think that they have. When you think about it, people have always killed people. Domestic violence is not new, wars are not new, assassination attempts are not new, killing is not new. What may be different now, however, is that through the media of television, radio, and the newspapers we have instant knowledge of what happens. We can read about it, hear about it, and, most of all, see it. Our in-depth knowledge of our world has increased; our capacity to see what happens in our world has widened. We are thrust into the middle of things in the world that formerly we stood a good distance from. Thus we are constantly stimulated with some of the horror that has always been a part of life. It is not that the horror is new. We just know and see more about it. It is much more a part of our lives.

In the face of this, how do people protect themselves? What happens, I fear, is that we begin to deaden ourselves. We begin to stop caring and stop feeling. It is not that anyone sets out to be hardened. It is just that when people are faced with one trauma after another they often become numbed, and lose touch with their capacity to feel and to care.

Under those circumstances, then, life itself becomes devalued. There are so many deaths in Northern Ireland, for instance, that who of us thinks twice anymore when we hear of another shooting, or hear of another hunger striker dying? That is the process of being hardened. There are so many shootings in and around Chicago that who of us thinks twice when we hear that another child has died? That is the process of being hardened.

It is in this world, however, that we live. It is to this world that we have been called. In his sermon at a special Mass called to pray for the health of the Pope, Cardinal Cody said that the incidents of terrorism and crimes of violence in the world have become all too common. Yet he also said, "We as Christians believe the world can be different." Peter said something similar: "But you are a chosen race, a royal priesthood, a holy nation, God's own people, that you may declare the wonderful deeds of him who called you out of darkness into his marvelous light." This is Peter's call to a mission which is exactly the opposite of our being hardened. This is Peter's call to us to be what God has already made us—His chosen people.

In the face of our inhumanity to each other, God's response was not to harden His heart; His response was not to turn His back; His response was not to despair; His response was not to hate. God's response was to continue to love and care for the world; God's response was to send His own Son to a violent death, that He might show His compassion for us.

It is out of God's love that each of us is here today. It is out of God's love that we are made God's own people.

It would not be too hard to think of God looking down on this world, seeing the violence and all that is in it, perceiving the small acts of uncaring we all do to each other. It would not be too hard to think of God shaking His head and going off to be God somewhere else, leaving us to our own problems with each other. But God does not leave. God stays. God calls us. God cares for us. God loves us.

Then it becomes our turn. All of us have our turn at life in our own small ways. In the schools where our young go, they are the holy nation; in the homes and neighborhoods where all of us live, we are God's own people there; in the workplace where we toil, we are a royal priesthood. We are called by God who has not turned His back on us not to turn our back on others; we are called by God who has cared for us to care for others, and to work to make the world different; we are called by God who has not hardened Himself to our cries not to harden ourselves to the cries of others; we are called by God who has loved us with an ever-lasting love to love others.

Surely we do this imperfectly. Surely we fail at being a royal priesthood. But in our imperfections God opens his arms to hold us. God empowers us not to harden our hearts. Jesus' words, "Truly, truly I say to you, whoever believes in me will do the works that I do," echo Peter's words, "You are a chosen race, a royal priesthood, a holy nation, God's own people, that you may declare the wonderful deeds of him who called you out of darkness into his marvelous light."

May we dare then hope? As people experience God's love, may we dare hope that a day will come when peace will reign, that a day will come when people will talk over their differences rather than act them out, that a day will come when no one would want to shoot a Pope, or anyone else for that matter?

THE CHURCH'S MINISTRY
IN A LONELY WORLD

Archie Smith, Jr., Ph.D.

Archie Smith, Jr., Ph.D., is an American Baptist pastor whose ministry has involved the integration of theology, psychology, and sociology. Currently Foster Professor of Pastoral Psychology and Counseling at Pacific School of Religion and a practicing marriage and family counselor in California, Dr. Smith also holds an M.S.W. and a Ph.D. in Sociology from Brandeis University. His work has involved ministry in local parishes and to the community, therapy in pastoral counseling centers, and teaching in a number of institutions of higher learning. His recent book The Relational Self: Ethics and Therapy from a Black Church Perspective *makes an important contribution toward the mating of personal and social transformation paradigms.*

Loneliness is the subject of his sermon published here, *The Church's Ministry in a Lonely World.* Without being academically didactic, Smith skillfully interweaves the personal, interpersonal, and communal aspects of this pervasive, powerful human predicament while focusing on the implications for Christian ministry.

I

It was another one of those demanding days at work. The phone seemed to ring constantly. There were frequent knocks at the door and the question, "Got a minute? I would like to bend your ear." I left early. Arrived home. Entered my study. Shut the door on the world, as it were, to begin another round of work. As I sat down at my desk, there in the quietness of my study, I focused on a prayer that hangs on the wall above the bookshelf. It goes something like this:

Slow me down, Lord. Ease the pounding of my heart by the quieting of my mind. Steady my hurried pace with a vision of the eternal reach of time. Give me, amid the confusion of the day, the calmness of the everlasting hills. Break the tensions of my nerves and muscles with the soothing music of the singing streams that live in my memory. Help me to know the magical restoring power of sleep. Teach me the art of taking minute vacations—of slowing down to look at a flower, to chat with a friend, to pat a dog, to read a few lines from a good book. Slow me down, Lord, and inspire me to send my roots deep into the soil of life's enduring values that I may grow toward the stars of my greater destiny.

I am often caught up short by this prayer that faces me each time I enter my study. My life so often seems to flow in the opposite direction of slowing down, as I feel the pressure of work and respond to the demands upon me and try to be a responsible person. How often are our lives like that—caught up by the demands and pressures upon us, subject to the evaluation of our peers and family members? Sometimes we *are* being judged, frequently being examined, and often questioned, if not by others, then certainly by ourselves ... "Now, why did I do that?" "Slow me down. . . ."

My sister and niece were visiting from Seattle. On one occasion, as I was feeling the pressure to hurry, my two-year-old niece reached out her tiny hand and we walked together. I had to slow down to match her tiny steps. It was not a question of whether she should keep pace with me, but could I slow down enough to keep pace with her? Somehow the prayer "Slow me down, Lord" was now conveyed through my two-year-old niece. She helped to put me in touch with my inner self. Our lives are often lived at a pace that is much too fast. And we find ourselves impatient with those who would go slower.

Think for a moment about the way many of us drive down the highway—as if it were our last trip; or the impatience that is so often shown on the faces of those who wait in toll lines during the "rush hours."

The story is told of a man who requested a taxi to come as soon as possible. When the taxi arrived, he rushed out of the door, jumped into the back seat and said, "Drive!" "Where to, sir?" asked the driver. "Anywhere," came the reply, "and hurry!"

Our hurried pace through life often bespeaks our anxiety about our loneliness by constantly seeking the company of others and by keeping continually busy, thus avoiding the crucial questions of life and death. To be human is to be aware of the reality of our loneliness.

It is often said that we are created for fellowship, for community. And we are. But we are also alone. In some very deep sense every creature is alone. And every person *knows* that he or she is alone. Our loneliness is something we cannot escape. It is a part of our destiny to be alone and to be aware of it. Consider a few ways that awareness of our loneliness comes through.

(1) We are often made aware of being alone in those moments when we feel misunderstood in spite of our best efforts to make ourselves understood.

(2) Loneliness is often evoked through feelings of guilt for not being who one is and not actualizing one's potentialities. (Moustakas)

(3) We are often aware of our aloneness and loneliness when our deep feelings of affection for someone are not shared or returned by him or her.

(4) We often feel our loneliness when our co-workers and family members or friends do not share our joys or sadness, or deepest convictions—and so, we stand alone.

(5) We often feel our isolation and loneliness when we have lost a dear friend or life companion. As one man recently put it to me, "I felt utterly alone when my wife and best friend of thirty-five years walked out on me."

(6) Sometimes we feel our loneliness even when surrounded by people or in a crowd. Sometimes we even feel our loneliness in churches where many people gather, but have little to do with each other. People can be lonely in isolation or lonely in a crowd; lonely because they have no one to be with or lonely

because they are with someone they can no longer reach. (Moustakas)

(7) We experience our loneliness and aloneness in our final journey—in our dying . . . a journey we must take alone.

Several years ago, I drove alone from Berkeley to Maine to Seattle and back to Berkeley. There were times when I was eager to talk to someone, to reach out and make contact. When I would stop for gas or coffee, I could usually tell who the other long distance drivers were. They were usually the ones who would walk up to the counter, initiate conversation, and who readily made small talk.

We live in a society in which loneliness has become one of the most painful human wounds. The growing competition and rivalry which pervade our lives from birth have created in us an acute awareness of our isolation. This awareness has in turn left many with a heightened anxiety and an intense search for the experience of unity and community. (Nouwen)

II

Last week's *New York Times Magazine* was devoted to the theme of loneliness. It pointed out that we Americans are ambivalent in our attitudes about loneliness. *On the one hand,* we have idealized the image of the "lonesome cowboy," the "private eye," the individual who has "the courage to stand alone." In school young people are taught to respect Thoreau for going without "companionship or society" at Walden Pond. The self-reliant, self-made individual who has found success without aid or comfort from others is held up as a cultural ideal. The many self-help books on best seller lists today are testimony to this idealized version of life.

On the other hand, loneliness has been linked with emotional disorders such as mental illness (most commonly depression), with alcohol and drug abuse, suicide, and physical disorders. Today, loneliness is recognized by many health professionals as a serious and growing problem for society. Some have even referred to loneliness as "epidemic" which can lead to self-destructive behavior.

More people live alone today than ever before. Marriage, the family, and community bonds that held people together in earlier times are now more easily dissolved. As one observer put it: "People no longer have communities to which they are irrevocably tied. Communities are brittle, fragile, with a tremendous turnover." (Bellah)

Shortly after my grandfather died last September at the age of one hundred and four, my sisters and brother and I wondered how my mother would fare in that big house alone. My brother stopped by one evening to look in on my mother, only to find her sitting alone staring into the fireplace with the television on in the background. She had not heard him enter the house.

Ordinary people cope with loneliness in ordinary ways. They keep the radio or the television on for company. They smile back at the anchorman or woman on the evening news when he or she says, "See you tomorrow." For companionship and society, they turn to soap operas that offer the illusion of involvement in other people's daily lives. People join churches, evangelical movements, or cults, buy things they don't really want, go to doctors more often than necessary and dial the weather report just to hear a friendly voice.

The San Francisco Bay area, where I live, is known for its singles bars, its matchmaking and video dating services, advertisements aimed at the lonely, and the proliferation of cults which promise salvation from loneliness. Increased loneliness is the inevitable outcome in any society where people are isolated more and more from belonging to something larger that would give them a sense of inclusion and fulfillment. People need to believe and feel that they have intrinsic worth and that they belong to a larger and meaningful fellowship.

Some years ago the Beatles used to sing: "All the lonely people, where do they all come from?" They come from everywhere. They are in families, our churches, schools, modern corporations, in rural and urban areas.

But loneliness need not be viewed solely as a negative experience. Loneliness can also be viewed as a condition which leads to deeper perception, greater awareness and sensitivity and insight. It has also led people to ask anew how love, friendship, brotherhood, sisterhood and peoplehood can free them from isolation and offer them a sense of intimacy and belonging that is not self-destructive. We need resources to facilitate greater awareness of the constructive possibilities in loneliness. *Can that resource come from the church and its ministry?*

III

The story is told of a nurse from Hartford, Connecticut, with cancer of the lung. She had come to the hospital as a patient. Two nights before the operation she asked that a minister (a representative of the church) be called. After the minister was seated at her bedside, she said, "I know what I have and how serious the operation is. I also know that the doctor can do only so much and that the patient must do the rest. I'm afraid I won't be able to do my part. That's why I wanted to see a pastor so that He can help me do my part."

The operation was unsuccessful. Two weeks later as the pastor stood at her bedside one night, she asked, "Do you think it will be tonight?" She referred to her approaching death. The pastor responded, "I don't know. Do you think it will?" "I don't know, but I want you to pray it will be. Only one thing more—I want you to come and be with my sister when it happens so she won't be alone." She died two nights later, and the pastor said, "I learned the lesson of the importance of pastoral prayer, for it was through prayer, quiet prayers with eyes closed and her hand clasped tightly in mine, that we groped for the strength she so desperately needed. She was aware of the reality of her loneliness. And, yet, she reached out in concern for her sister even as she was ministered unto."

Christian ministry today may well be characterized by the themes of loneliness, reaching out, and burden bearing. Ministers are challenged to enable others to be burden bearers for Christ's sake. I want to suggest that the church, as an intentional community, has a role to play, a ministry to perform in a lonely world. By "ministry" I have in mind the *ministry of the laity*. The congregation as a whole and each member has a ministry. For a long time churches have thought of the professional clergy as being the ones responsible for the church's ministry. But lately there has been increased recognition of the role of the laity, the members of the congregation, as having a ministry as well.

The story is told of a young woman whose husband deserted, leaving her to raise their four children singlehanded. Raising four children singlehanded was very difficult. Soon she learned that she had cancer. That revelation was like the last straw. She became quite depressed. She signed herself into a hospital and determined that she would die. She refused food and went from one hundred and forty pounds to ninety-seven pounds. Her life had become unbearable and she came to believe that no one really cared about her. And there she lay in a hospital bed dying and without the will to live. She had given up.

A nurse's aide who worked the midnight shift noticed this woman who had given up. Late at night when the hospital became quiet, the room lights were turned off and most patients were asleep, this nurse's aide would quietly slip into the young lady's room, sit at her bedside, talk to her, read a few familiar passages of scripture, pray, and quietly hum a spiritual. As she did this, the patient slowly regained her desire to live again. Eventually the young lady left the hospital and to this day is doing quite well. No one will ever know who was this nurse's aide. But what we do know is that her faith and ministry was a source of healing. *She helps us to see what powerful ministries lay people can have.* Ordained clergy and laity together comprise the whole ministry of Christ's church in the world.

We can take seriously the encouragement of the philosopher William Ernest Hocking, "We have no choice but to be involved in loneliness—to immerse ourselves in the stream of history and to accept our time-location." (This is a paraphrase.) These are times of deep-felt loneliness, isolation and suffering. In times such as these, the church can be a caring community which seeks to nurture the worth, dignity and growth of people. The call to community is of paramount importance in a society that puts high emphasis on personal freedom, autonomy and independence and individualism. The call to community is a call to responsibility, a call to "bear one another's burdens." It is a call to recognize that we are "members one of another."

To bear one another's burdens means to listen with openness and without manipulation to another. This is difficult. To listen attentively and without manipulation is to make possible open and honest relationships. It permits us to be with people as they actually are, and not as we wish they were. This is difficult work.

Open listening is difficult, for what we often hear is painful and sometimes shocking. But if people are to experience genuine acceptance, then they must be allowed to risk sharing who they deeply feel themselves to be in the presence of another.

Genuine listening is difficult because we are often confronted with material we find hard to hear. The story is told of a church member who made a call on a church family. The family was experiencing some difficulties with their younger daughter and wanted to talk about their difficulties with a person they felt cared about them. But the church member kept diverting the conversation to a lighter topic centered around his own needs. It soon became clear that he was unwilling or unable to listen to the family's pain and soon he left.

Sometimes what people need most from us is to just listen and to give them the opportunity to share their burden. This may be called a ministry of effective listening.

There is another word that is an ingredient in the church's ministry. That word is solitude. Solitude is not easy either. It is the capacity to be alone without being lonely. It is a voluntary turning inward and centering so that we can discover the rich resources that lie deep within us. It is out of solitude that real ministry can happen. It was the contemplative, Robert Merton, who said, "If you would rescue another, you can't just throw yourself into the stream with him or her. You may be pulled under the current too. You have to have a place on which to stand—a resource and an anchor."

In solitude, we can nurture the inner resources which are the stuff of ministry. Clark Moustakas suggested: "In real solitude, we are expansive, limitless, free. We do not disguise our feelings from ourselves, but rather we renew contact with ourselves and discover who we are." Solitude, then, is a return to one's own self when the world has grown cold and meaningless, when life has become filled with people and too much of a response to others.

When we turn inward and center down, we can become aware that there is a dialogue going on inside. Sometimes words fail us, but somehow we come to discover that there are deep treasures within. We may even find meaning in the Psalmist's discovery:

> Whither shall I go from thy Spirit?
> or whither shall I flee from thy presence?
> If I ascend to heaven, thou art there!
> If I make my bed in hell, thou art there.
> If I take the wings of the morning
> and dwell in the uttermost parts of the sea,
> Even there thy hand shall lead me,
> and thy right hand shall hold me. (Psalm 139:7-9)

I called this a discovery because this depth awareness results from solitude. It is not surface wisdom. It is an awakening and comes from contact with the ultimate mystery of life.

Solitude makes possible effective listening, trust and open sharing. This is at the heart of ministry. In solitude we discover ourselves as genuine resources for the healing of others; and other people are essential to the recovery of our own humanity.

As an intentional community, we learn to value people, not our possessions or status. As a listening community, we learn to share one another's burdens. As a community of faith, we work to be effective ministers, but we are not destroyed by the lack of results. And as a community of faith, we remind one another constantly that we form a caring fellowship, a presence that may be a source of healing and new life in the midst of a lonely world. Now, the sermon is concluded, but your ministry must commence!

A BLESSING FOR ME

Henry T. Close, Th.M.

*Well known as a gifted therapist and teacher, and well pub-
lished in therapeutic circles, Henry Close is a Diplomate in
the American Association of Pastoral Counselors. He is currently working as a pastoral therapist in Florida after many
years on the staff of the Georgia Mental Health Clinic in
Atlanta.*

The deep and powerful desire to be blessed by one's parent is
the subject of his sermon *A Blessing for Me.* He uses the blessing story in the Old Testament involving Jacob, Esau, and
their father Isaac, as well as contemporary illustrations to deal
with this important, though oft-neglected subject.

A few years ago I had the opportunity of supervising part of the
training of a middle-age minister who was working on his doctor-
ate in theology at one of the theological seminaries in Atlanta. In
the process of working together, we became rather close. It was
clear that he had had a very hard time of it in the process of growing up. The family was poor to begin with, and then his father
died when he was quite young. So his mother had given herself to
holding the family together. By some very hard work and with the
help of God, she saw every one of her children through high school
and college—every one except Robert.

Robert was the black sheep of the family. He was the young-
est and in many ways he had suffered the most from his father's
death. His mother's working had meant that he was deprived of
some very important mothering when he needed it the most, and
he reacted by failing at everything he undertook. He dropped out
of high school, got into drugs and alcohol very heavily—especially
alcohol—was involved in a series of petty crimes, spent time in
prison, and so forth. Finally his wife took their four kids and left,
which pushed him even further into despair.

During all this time, though, his mother stood by him. She
had faith in him. Finally something happened and he managed to

turn the corner to begin the long hard struggle of building a new life for himself. He finished school, worked his way through college, and then theological seminary, and was to be ordained to the gospel ministry. I think he was the first person from his community ever to enter the ministry, so the ordination was a really big event. The service was to be in his home church in the small town where he had grown up, the scene of all the struggles, the defeats, the humiliation—and now the triumph. The church was filled with people who knew him and knew what he had been through.

As part of the ordination service his mother had been asked to say something relative to the occasion. Robert wondered of course what she would say. Would she comment on the faithfulness of God? On the depth of people's struggles? On the importance of not giving up? On the reality of new beginnings? What? When she stood, she walked to the pulpit and said very simply with tears in her voice, "This is my beloved son, in whom I am well pleased."

Now this was what Jacob and Esau wanted from their father. They wanted him to bless them. They longed for that deep powerful affirmation from their father that would say to them from the depth of his soul, "You are my son, in whom I am well pleased."

There are a lot of things we don't understand about this encounter between Jacob and Esau and their father Isaac. We just don't know what the customs were back then. Why could not Isaac bless both his sons instead of just the one? Why the ritual of the meal? Why wait until his death-bed to bless his sons? We just don't know. But the emotional urgency and anguish of the situation—that is clear. It is one of the universal themes of our human drama. The hunger of a son—or a daughter—for a parent's blessing: we can all understand the poignancy of that yearning. The blessing is the same in its emotional impact regardless of which parent it comes from. And if the blessing is not there, there is something missing, unfinished, in the depth of our lives. The blessing was so important to Jacob—even though he obviously had his mother's blessing—that he would resort to anything to get his father's blessing. He was willing to lie; he was even willing to accept it fraudently while impersonating his brother. People don't do that kind of thing unless the longing is very deep and very strong.

What is this blessing that is so important? What does it consist of? How do we understand its personal significance for our lives?

We don't have a formal definition of the blessing. It has something to do with the quality of the relationship a parent has with a child. It is a deep-seated affirmation, approval, of the child by the parent. It's more than love, even. It is like a voice from deep in the parent's soul that says, "You're O.K. You are my son, my daughter. I'm proud to have you as mine, to invest my life in you. You are my beloved child, with whom I am well pleased." It's more than words can ever express, of course. And it is something that every one of us has wanted from his or her parents. Do you remember the older brother of the prodigal son? His younger brother was the one who had obviously had his father's blessing. When the brother finally returned home, his father celebrated with a great feast. The older brother remonstrated with his father. "I've been a faithful son. I've stayed with you to do my job. I've been responsible. I've always done everything you wanted. Why have you never celebrated my life? Why have you never blessed me?" It sounds like Esau crying out, "Don't you have even one blessing for me?"

I think it is worthwhile to think back to your own family and the kinds of blessings that occurred there. Who was it in your family who blessed you? Who was it who gave you that sparkle in their eye, who took delight in you, so that you really knew that you were a beloved son or daughter in whom they were well pleased? Who was it who blessed you? Mother? Father? Maybe an older brother or sister, or aunt or uncle? Maybe even a neighbor or teacher or pastor? I know that for me, when I was very young and my parents were pressuring me to be perfect, it was my grandfather who simply liked me. I still think of that as one of the most important influences in my life.

But the blessing is not always forthcoming. In some cases it is blocked off fairly completely. Some parents just don't have it in them to bless their children. If they could, they would, yet sometimes—for whatever reasons—they just can't. But the resulting lack of blessing can feel really overwhelming, and can drive people to do desperate things, sometimes. It's like an emptiness we carry within us that pushes us in ways we may not understand, pushing us to find something to make up for the lack of blessing. So what do we do with the unblessed part of us? What happens when the blessing is not forthcoming?

The first thing to realize is that it is as much a loss to the parents as it is to the child. To bless our children is an integral part of being a parent, of feeling like a parent.

When a parent can't bless his/her children, the feeling of being a parent is compromised; it is unfinished, unfulfilled. I know for myself when I look at my kids with delight, when there is a sparkle in my eye for them, it's then that I really feel like a father. But when I'm angry or out of sorts, preoccupied—when the blessing is being withheld—I don't feel that sense of wholeness as a parent. It is a loss to the parents to not be able to bless.

It is also a loss to the kids. It is an emptiness they experience too, a sense of being unfulfilled as children. There is something unfinished, incomplete. When it is really strong, people may do some rather extreme things to deal with it. Take Esau, for instance. The first thing he did after being denied his father's blessing was to go and marry a Caananite woman—something he knew would displease his father. He was angry, and was going to get even. Or closer to home, we have witnessed the near tragedy that happened when President Reagan was shot in Washington. Apparently here was a young man so hungry, so desperate that he was willing to kill and be killed for a blessing from a young actress that was at best imaginary, from a person he had never even met—a very desperate hunger.

At the other extreme are people who react with despair. It's as though life doesn't really mean as much as it should. To feel unblessed can carry with it some pretty strong feelings of unworthiness and inadequacy. It's easy to feel that it's just not worth trying.

But probably what most of us do to deal with the lack of blessing is to look for it elsewhere.

We can easily bring the hunger to be blessed to our work, and endow that with a compulsive drive to succeed. "If my parents can't bless me, maybe my work can." But the blessing we seek doesn't come from impersonal sources, in response to our achievements. It comes from persons, in response to our soul. "I don't want you to love me for my achievements; I want you to love me for me."

Or we can bring the hunger to our social relationships. People have been known to go from one relationship to another to another—often empty or even destructive relationships—searching frantically for some kind of blessing. But it is easy to invest that kind of hunger unwisely and make yourself vulnerable to the wrong people. Instead of finding blessing, you may find pain and disillusionment.

Or we bring the hunger to our marriages. I think it is one of the things that motivates people to marry. We seek some*one* who can bless us. But if we ask too much of a marriage, if we place on it the impossible demand that it fully satisfy our hunger to be blessed, then we over-burden the marriage and it can wither and die.

Or we bring the hunger back to our parents with a renewed kind of determination. It's easy for kids to think that if they can just please their parents better, then they will be blessed. Do you remember Tennessee Williams' play, "Cat on a Hot Tin Roof"? The oldest son, Brick, was like the prodigal son's older brother, desperately trying to get his father's blessing. At one point he remonstrated with his father: "You told me to get married; I got married. You told me to have a child; I had a child. You told me to become a lawyer; I became a laywer. What do I have to do to please you?"

If your parents can't bless you, they can't bless you. And nothing you can do will change that.

At other times we bring the need to be blessed directly to God. We think of God as Father, and to open our lives, our feelings to Him is to ask for the blessing. And there are rare moments in life when we feel our hearts strangely warmed as we kneel to His presence. We know that we really do matter to God, that we're important to Him, and we are able to feel and receive His blessing.

But the blessing from God doesn't take away our need to be blessed by our family. It fills a very special need, but God has made us so that we need other people also. He blesses, and that blessing gives us a new courage and wisdom as we look for other blessings as well. Usually, His blessing is channeled through other people.

When a person does find this blessing that he hungers for, it doesn't solve all his problems or guarantee that he will have a good life. Jacob is an example. Even though he received the blessing, his life was full of difficulty and problems. What the blessing does is to set the child free to be his own person. It satisfies a kind of deep yearning in a person that has to be met if he is to get beyond that and really be free to be himself. Once that quest is finished, there is a new freedom to find one's place in the world.

Part of being one's own person is that the blessed person can become a source, a channel of blessing to other people. We pass the blessing along to other people—to our children, and, perhaps on occasion, to our neighbor—or even to our parents. This was Jesus' ministry. He of course was uniquely blessed by His heavenly Father, and His ministry was full of blessing for other people. Even Jacob, whose blessing was flawed, became the channel of blessing for the people of God. The blessed person becomes the channel of blessing for others. It's especially rich when it is able to come full circle, and we realize he has the power to bless his own parents.

I mentioned my friend Robert. After a few years in the ministry, he met and fell in love with a lovely woman, and decided to get married. Robert had been married once and had children, and he had been a lousy husband and father. So it was with much anxiety that he entered into a second marriage, wondering if he would fail at it this time too.

The woman he married had a ten-year-old daughter Debbie who really resented Robert. She had had mom all to herself for several years and she didn't want any intruder coming between them. So from the very beginning she tried to break the relationship up. She avoided Robert, pouted at him, refused to have anything to do with him, snapped at him, was constantly angry and resentful. Of course this fed all the feelings he had anyhow of being a lousy father, and hurt him pretty deeply. But he had enough maturity by this time so that he didn't punish her for it; he didn't push himself on her or demand that she straighten up. He just quietly kept on being there, reaching out to her very gently, being as loving as he could, even though it still hurt every time she rejected him. One day at a school picnic for kids and parents, Debbie met a new friend and brought her over to introduce her to her mother. Robert as usual stepped aside and didn't interfere. They talked with her mother for a few seconds. Then Debbie turned to Robert and for the first time said with a kind of warm pride in her voice, "This is my daddy."

He managed not to cry, but he felt those four words to be overwhelming. He knew that finally he had been accepted, he had been *blessed!* And you and I have that same power with our parents, just as we as parents have that power with our children.

Ultimately, all blessing comes from God. We don't generate it, we participate in it. It emanates from God Himself, is mediated through other people, and comes to rest for a while on you and me. Then we pass it on to our children or our parents or sometimes to someone else. The blessing expresses itself in the loving affirmation, "I'm proud to have you as my child," or in the words of Jesus, "Well done, good and faithful servant." The blessing then sets people free to be their own persons, hopefully to be channels of blessing for other people, especially for their children, or for their parents. Something really important happens in our souls when we truly hear and truly speak the blessing, "This is my beloved child, in whom I am well pleased."

PRAYER: *We are humbled, Lord, by the power of someone's blessing. And as we give thanks, we ask for receptive and generous hearts to be able to receive and to pass on to another the blessing that ultimately comes from Thee. In the name of Christ. Amen.*

THE ADVENT
OF GIANTS

Luke 5:1–11
First Sunday in Advent
(Communion)

Gregory J. Johanson

In *The Advent of Giants,* preached in the normal course of the lectionary, Johanson (see biographical note preceding *Be Angry But Do Not Sin*) uses a series of literary, personal, and scriptural examples which illustrate Runyon's principle of speaking from strength to strength. It appeared in modified form as "Raising the Giant Within You" in *Pulpit Resource,* Vol. 5, No. 3, 1977.

A colleague of mine, Ray Balcomb [to whom I am indebted for this initial Coleridge-Wordsworth illustrative material] of First United Methodist Church of Portland, Oregon, says that if your high school or college English courses were like his, you would have been taught a certain respect for the English poet and thinker, Samuel Taylor Coleridge.

I personally did not get in on as much literature as I would have liked to in school, so I took the opportunity this week to go back and read some of Coleridge that I had missed in the past. It was not hard to affirm that his use of blank-verse poems, or what he called his "conversation poems," which integrally related meditation and description, were beautifully done in such poems as *Frost at Midnight:*

The Frost performs its secret ministry,
Unhelped by any wind. . . .
'Tis calm indeed! so calm, that it disturbs
And vexes meditation with its strange
and extreme silentness. Sea, hill, and wood,
This populance village! Sea, and hill, and wood,
With all the numberless goings-on of life,
Inaudible as dreams!

With all the respect that we are accustomed to accord Coleridge, it might be a bit of a shock to find out that more recent scholarship has claimed that he has been rather overrated, that

84

perhaps much of his stuff is second or third rate, short on creative originality, and heavy on "borrowing" from others. Even the most severe critics concede however that he produced a handful of works which represent major achievements of genius and originality. "The Ancient Mariner," "Kubla Khan," and "Frost at Midnight" are recognized in particular as going beyond the capability of any mediocre talent.

The explanation which is given for how Coleridge could have had such a burst of creativity, producing such undeniably great works, is that during the time he wrote them he was in a very close and supportive relationship with an even greater poet, William Wordsworth. It is said:

> Nearly everything that counts in Coleridge's performance as a poet sprang . . . from a symbiotic (that is, living, vital, supportive) relation with . . . Wordsworth's guiding hand, both formally and technically. . . . It is Wordworth's radical novel vision of natural language and of nature, together with Dorothy Wordsworth's inspired eye for landscape and weather, that transforms the young S.T.C. from a stilted, markedly derivative . . . versifier into a seer of strange beauty.

To say this in another way, the flowering of Coleridge's talents in 1797 came about through the influence of a close and deep relationship with one whom Coleridge wrote of in this way to a friend in June 1797: "I speak with heartfelt sincerity, and (I think) unblinded judgment, when I tell you that I feel myself a little man by his side."

"A little man by his side." To use a different image, Coleridge thought of Wordsworth as *a giant*. And I think we all know what having our personal giants is about. Giants are people whom we gravitate toward because they seem to have something that we feel we lack, something that makes them special because of our not sharing it with them. And for some reason we want to be around them because we have some fantasy or hope that maybe they can give us some of what they have, or that what we desire will rub off on us through association. Coleridge apparently benefited from rubbing shoulders with his giant Wordsworth, though let us keep in mind the point right now that it did not last; it did not seem to become part of him.

There are many examples of "personal giant stories." In the Old Testament story in 2 Kings we remember that Elijah before his death asks of his friend and prodigy Elisha, "What shall I do for you, before I am taken from you?" and Elisha responds, "I pray you, let me inherit a double share of your spirit."

I would like to share with you now the story of an encounter I had with one of the giants of my own life. This man was both one of my pastoral supervisors and a pastoral counselor that my wife and I benefited from greatly. I had looked up to him in many ways for his sensitivity, his care, insight, ability to be both honest and helpful with people, and so forth. While I had been doing a lot of growing and maturing during the time I knew him, I still felt in many ways like a "little man by his side," that I was far from being where he was at. He was definitely one of my giants.

But then the last time I saw him before coming back from seminary and training, he actually helped me acknowledge with him openly that he was in fact one of my giants—something people don't usually share with each other freely. And he pushed the issue by asking me what in particular it might be about him that I valued so. The response which I remember best is that I told him I envied him most his *warmth*—the tremendous way he could affirm people while being so straight and "non-syrupy" with them.

At this point he completely turned the process around. "My warmth?" he asked, "You think you experience my warmth?" "Yes," I said. "That's right." "No," he responded, "there is no way you can possibly experience my warmth. My warmth is mine. That is *your warmth* you are experiencing inside you!" I was literally struck to the core and I still am every time I experience the moment again in my memory. What an incredible gift. My giant had dethroned himself by enthroning me, by making it clear that we were both more alike than different, that his spirit could touch my spirit, but that there was no way I could sense or experience something in him that was not in me. We both had been created with common basic resources by God. The reason he was appropriately my supervisor was that he was farther along in his pilgrimage of redeeming and learning to use his resources or gifts, and was skilled in encouraging myself and others in our pilgrimages. That encounter is something I carry with me to this day, and the significance and meaning of it has grown in me continuously.

And now this morning I am prepared to make a comparison for our instructional purposes, and say that this encounter of mine which I related is a closer approximation of that between Jesus and Peter which we read today than what we know on the surface of the encounter between Coleridge and Wordsworth.

Coleridge, it seems, took Wordsworth to be a giant right from the start, and apparently Wordsworth responded by assuming this role and maintaining it, inspiring Coleridge when they were together and leaving him high and dry when they were apart. My friend, in contrast, responded by calling to the giant in me. He did not give up any of his personal greatness, but he was concerned to touch those same elements in me so that we might both have them available. This is analogous to what Jesus did with Peter in our story from Luke.

Peter experiences Jesus for the first time beside the Lake of Gennesaret. He is ultimately overwhelmed by Jesus' presence which also touches his fear, and he falls down at Jesus' feet and says, "Depart from me for I am a sinful man, O Lord." Peter acknowledges Jesus as a giant indeed. But Jesus' response is to call to the giant *in Peter*. He does not say to Peter, "True, you are nothing by yourself; you only catch fish by the merits of your association with me." He says in effect, "True, I am a catcher of persons, but do not be afraid; henceforth *you* will be catching people." He calls to the giant in Peter. And he continues to do so throughout the gospel. He says things like: "There is truly a rock in me and there is also a rock within your seemingly shifting sand, Peter, on which I will depend to build my church." He tells Peter, "I have endeavored to feed my flock; now if you love me, you feed my sheep; you can do it."

What I finally want to say on this First Sunday in Advent, looking forward to the birth of Christ at Christmas, is that Jesus also calls to the giant *in us*. We so often, and appropriately, look forward to the birth of the Christ Child as the birth of new hope in an old world. But what I want us to consider is that if the Christ

Child represents new hope, the revelation of the divine in human form, and the revelation of what it truly means to be human when filled with the divine spirit—which we affirm it does—then the real hope for the world is that Christ's spirit can touch our spirits and therefore spread in incarnate form throughout the world. It is not sufficient that Christmas simply be the advent of a single giant. It must be the beginning of the advent of many giants, a multitude of giants. We, like Peter, must be sensitive to Christ's call, "Follow me."

And we do hear the call. "You are the salt of the earth," says Jesus. "You are the light of the world." Do not despair because I am leaving you, he tells us, because greater things than these shall you do.

Let us think about our calling as giants then, as we come to communion this morning. If we think that the birth of Christ is so hopeful because of the warmth and affirmation and love He brought into the world, then let us think about how He calls us to discover and use those same things in ourselves. If it is His strength or sensitivity or transparency to the Divine or whatever that impresses us, again, let us think about these things in relation to ourselves and in relation to our neighbor kneeling beside us. Let us think about the advent of giants this Advent-Christmas season, and let us give thanks. Amen.

IDENTITY CONFIRMED
Glenn E. Whitlock, Ph.D.

Glenn E. Whitlock is a United Presbyterian pastor who served as a parish minister and university chaplain before contracting polio and subsequently studying for a Ph.D. in Clinical Psychology. He is currently Professor of Psychology at the experimental Johnston College of the University of Redlands, Adjunct Professor at San Francisco Theological Seminary, a consultant for a community crisis hot line, and counselor with a Christian counseling service. He has published three books, numerous journal articles and finds time to enjoy family, friends, and leisure activities.

His profound integration of theology and psychology are reflected in his sermon *Identity Confirmed* that deals with the ever current issue of identity. In it he masterfully relates the subject both to the classic Christian doctrines of hope and grace, and the wonderful children's story of the Velveteen Rabbit. The sermon was preached at the United Church of Christ in Redlands, California, July 26, 1981, while that congregation was in the process of calling a new minister.

"Therefore, since we are justified by faith, we have peace with God through our Lord Jesus Christ." (Romans 5:1, RSV)

Years ago in my first pastorate, I learned to respect the profound simplicity of children's stories. Perhaps it was the early memory of stories read and related to me as a child that provided the basis of my judgment. At any rate, in telling stories as part of the "Children's Sermon," I noticed the profound insights that were embedded in many of these stories. And I was impressed by two specific observations. First, the children were attentive to every word of the stories, and their alert responses signified their learning. Second, and to my initial surprise, adults in the congregation often referred to the points of the stories, and sometimes referred to them more readily than to points laboriously developed by the young minister who was learning to preach in his first pulpit.

Along with this respect for the simple truths in some children's stories, I now experience the joy of reading and telling stories to my own children. Several years ago, I discovered Margery Williams Bianco's delightful story, "The Velveteen Rabbit." For those of you who have already read this story to your children, you may remember that this rabbit was the plaything of a little boy who had come to love him and who carried him around even as my daughter carries her Teddy Bear around our house. When he was very new, the little rabbit had a spotted brown and white coat and real thread whiskers. He had a few proud moments when the boy discovered him on Christmas morning, but he was soon neglected because of all the other toys that the little boy received. The Velveteen Rabbit felt inferior to the more expensive toys, and they snubbed him. Only the Skin Horse, who had been in the nursery longer than any of the other toys, was kind to him. The Skin Horse was so old that his brown coat was bald in patches and his seams showed, but he was wise and he understood about nursery magic.

One day the Velveteen Rabbit asked the Skin Horse, "What is real? Does it mean having things that buzz inside you and a stick-out handle?" The Skin Horse replied, "Real isn't how you are made, it's a thing that happens to you. When a child loves you for a long, long time, not just to play with, but really loves you, then you become real."

The question of the Velveteen Rabbit is precisely the question that human beings ask: "What does it mean to be real?" And the answer is, of course, that we become real when we are loved. We are defined as real by those persons who love us, and by God who loves us. The late Lex Miller of Stanford University once remarked, "You don't know who you are until someone tells you." All of us need significant other persons to help us become real, to be told who we are. We need parents and friends to tell us that we are accepted—that we are loved.

Biblical faith affirms this simple insight. In one of the most profound theological discussions in any literature, Paul writes the simple message to the Romans that since we are accepted, we have peace with God. He writes, "While we were yet helpless, at the right time, Christ died for the ungodly." (Romans 5:6 RSV) Paul is simply saying that God loves us—that He accepts us as we are right now. And it is this acceptance that tells us who we are. We are real! Our identity is confirmed. An artist once remarked that the function of an artist is to remind people of who they are. In the same sense, the function of biblical faith is to remind us who we are. We are real. Our identity as real persons is confirmed by God's love for us.

The purpose of biblical faith is to remind us of our potentialities as human beings, to remind us of what it really means to be human. Any commitment of ourselves that results in less than the realization of our total potential is a form of idolatry. Achieving only a part of our potential as persons as the result of a limited commitment means that our god is too small. Our identity as loved by God is a free and unlimited affirmation that we are real; our identity is confirmed.

Granted, the problem of discovering identity is not a simple matter. It *is* a simple insight, but it may be difficult to actualize in experience. Some people apparently try to discover a sense of identity from the expectations of others. They are not looking at *acceptance* offered by others, but they are listening to the *expectations* of others. When people talk about who they are and what they expect from life, it is often startling to discover that it is not their own goals they are talking about. They often talk about what their parents, employers or professors expect of them. Rollo May related that one person said, "I am just a collection of mirrors, reflecting what everyone expects of me." He related the experience of one such "mirror person." A young woman could not make up her mind about which young man to marry—a safe young man with middle-class values who was approved by her family, or a man with whom she shared exciting interests, a man of imagination and creativity. While the latter young man was most attractive to her, he did not represent social and financial security. During the period of her indecision, she dreamed of a large gathering of people who took a vote on which of the two men to marry. During the dream she felt relieved. The solution was certainly convenient. The only trouble was that when she awoke, she couldn't remember which way the vote had gone.

These "empty" persons are described by T.S. Eliot who wrote long ago in 1925:

> We are the hollow men.
> We are the stuffed men
> Learning together, headpiece filled with straw.
> Alas, shape without form,
> Shade without color
> Paralyzed force, gesture without motion.

In his book *The Lonely Crowd,* David Riessman points out that the same dynamics are present in the American character. He suggests that many Americans tend to be "outer directed." These persons do not seek to be outstanding, but to fit in. They live as though they were directed by a radar set fastened to their heads, perpetually telling them what other people expect of them. These persons get their motives and directions from others. They are able to react against someone, but they are not able to initiate action on their own or to choose a goal on their own and commit themselves to it.

The only trouble is that no one ever discovers a sense of one's identity from the expectations of others. Attempting to reach our goals by that route, we are bound to discover that we are on a dead-end street. We only discover we are real by being loved. And our identity is confirmed as we experience acceptance and love as we are—without any expectations. When the little boy said to the Velveteen Rabbit that he wasn't a toy, but that he was real, that he was loved, "then the little rabbit didn't mind how he looked to other people because the nursery magic had made him real. And when you are real, shabbiness doesn't matter."

From the biblical perspective, Paul writes to the Romans, "But God shows His love for us in that while we were yet sinners Christ died for us." (Romans 5:8 RSV) Now it's unusual news to hear about anyone sacrificing his life even for a good person. But here Christ is reported dying for us while we were yet sinners. While we are unworthy, God accepts us as we are. We don't have to make "Brownie points" with God to win His acceptance. Biblical faith affirms that God loves us despite what we are. He simply accepts us, and hence we know who we are. Our identity is confirmed. We are real!

Hence, it is through God's acceptance of us that we discover our identity. We really are God's people as we are loved by Him. And as God's people, it is our hope to share in God's gifts. In this same biblical record, Phillip's translation of Paul's words reads, "Through Him we have confidently entered into this new relationship of grace, and here we take our stand, in happy certainty of the glorious things He has in store for us in the future." (Romans 5:2) Paul's reference to hope relates to our identity as God's people.

Our attitude toward *hope* indicates our attitude toward *life* and confirmation of our identity. In Eugene O'Neill's play, "The Iceman Cometh," the people in Harry Hope's barroom all live by false hopes until the iceman comes and destroys their illusions, and challenges them to go out and to face the real world. They have lived so long with their false hopes that they are unable to face reality. They fall back into their hellish existence by returning to their false hopes. The woman who felt she could make a great success on the stage was reminded that this hope was false. Nevertheless, she returned to her false hope because she could not live with the reality of her limited talent.

In interpersonal relations, this identical situation is represented in the game that Eric Berne identified as "If it weren't for you." In it, a woman married a man who dominated her and refused to let her work outside the home. She said to her husband, "If it weren't for you, I could go out and work and have a career." All the while, she is afraid of competition in a career, and she is unaware that she is unconsciously asking her husband to protect her from such competition and the possibility of failure. Her husband fulfills his part of this unconscious "game" by dominating her and insisting that she stay at home. She purposely—albeit unconsciously—married a man who dominates her and keeps her safe from competition and fear of failure. At the same time, she lives with the false hope that "if it weren't for you, I could achieve my goal of a career."

While "false hope" maintains a sense of unreality that continues a pattern of evasion of life, genuine hope opens us to vulnerability. In this hope we are vulnerable to hurt and disappointment. False hope does not involve vulnerability precisely because illusions block out the possibility of disappointment and failure. Christian hope involves vulnerability because it is not a matter of "pie in the sky, bye and bye." This hope is a reality that begins here and now. In Phillip's translation, Paul suggests, "This doesn't mean, of course, that we have only a hope of future joys—we can be full of joy here and now, even in our trials and troubles." (Romans 5:3-5) To the Christian, hope is both a present and a future reality. It is akin to both the Christmas that is a present reality in the spirit prior to December 25, and that which is finally only realized on December 25.

Christian hope, then, is related to the Christian affirmation of identity. It begins with the affirmation that God loves us as we are without our having to earn that love. It continues with God's continuing love, even in our disobedience. It is this hope of God's continuing love that affirms our identity, and this hope is a process. It usually doesn't happen all at once.

The Skin Horse told the Velveteen Rabbit that becoming real doesn't happen all at once. "You become. It takes a long time. That's why it doesn't often happen to people who break easily or have sharp edges or who have to be carefully kept. Generally, by the time you are real most of your hair has been loved off and your eyes drop out and you get loose in the joints and very shabby. But these things don't matter at all, because once you are real you can't be ugly except to people who don't understand."

To be identified with Christ, then, involves being incorporated into a new humanity. We are, then, identified as "new beings." "New beings" include new self-understanding. Such new self-understanding is akin to the instance of the brash young man who always thought he was "God's gift to women," until the time he fell in love with a beautiful young woman. Then he reflected, "What in the world can she see in me?"

With this new self-understanding, we are able to respond differently. With our identity confirmed, we are able to respond to another's need. Once we experience the security of knowing who we are, we no longer need to anxiously wander like amnesia victims who do not know who they are. With our identity confirmed, we can finally get on with our lives. We are now free from the anxiety about ourselves to be able to respond to somebody else's need.

Now when I talk about responsibility to one another, I am not referring to still another obligation that we "ought" to fulfill. I am not suggesting that we "ought" to be a man or woman for others. It is not so much an *obligation* as it is a *possibility*. The word responsibility means precisely what it says, *response-able*. Being a person for others is not so much a requirement for a Christian as it is a *possibility* for persons who know who they are and are secure and free enough to be there for others.

I am not suggesting that loving others is without risk. It's beautiful to love and to be a person for others, but it is risky business. John Fry, one-time pastor of First Presbyterian Church in Chicago, once remarked: "The most dangerous thing you can do is to love. The world isn't ready for it. Greed it can manage, lust it can understand, hate it thrives on, meanness makes it go around, but the world is enraged by love. So, grow up and watch out." And if we need any further warning, recall that Jesus was crucified because He dared to love in a radical sense.

But while it's risky business to love and care for others, it is evidence of vitality and aliveness. To fail to respond to love and care for others is a failure in being a genuine human being, and it represents a failure in being one in Christ. Failure to respond with love is a failure in courage—a failure in aliveness. Loving does call for courage because it is risky business, but in loving you show aliveness and power.

Having our identity confirmed as loved by God means that we are *real*. Being *real* means that we are able to respond as Jesus responded to others. It is a response that results from love in much the same sense that a beautiful sunset results in our response to that awesome beauty. And if a person doesn't respond, that's his or her problem. And if you don't respond to being loved by loving others, that's your problem. If you don't respond, that's your loss.

Failure to respond to love says, "I don't know who I am, so I'm afraid to love." *Identity unknown.*

Responding to love says, "I know who I am. I know I am one of God's people, and I am involved in the world that God loves and cares for." Responding means that I am *able* to be alive to myself and to the world which God has given us, and in which we live and work. *Identity confirmed.*

FREEDOM
AND LIMITATIONS
Reuel L. Howe, S.T.D.

One person who is held in warm esteem in the pastoral care world and can be appropriately considered a "pastor's pastor" is Reuel L. Howe. He is probably best known as the founder and director of the interdenominational Institute for Advanced Pastoral Studies at Bloomfield Hills, Michigan and for his clear, concise, never dull books relating theological and psychological insights to everyday life. Certainly in his teaching, supervising, and workshop leading he has been experienced as one who incarnates in his person the concepts that he writes and talks about. This quality of aliveness, of being encountered, is evident in his sermon published here.

Freedom and Limitations is the mature product of the many years of pastoral wisdom of Howe, richly illustrated with examples from his personal life. He expounds the meaning of "the Spirit of the Lord" in life as well as the freedom that can be achieved through a creative use of limitations.

"Where the spirit of the Lord is, there is freedom."
(2 Corinthians 3:17)

When I was a youth I dreamed of being twenty-one years old and therefore free. I wanted to be free of parental control and I fought that control in both legal and illegal ways. I wanted to be free of having to do homework, and my rebellion against it cost me the loss of a respectable academic record. I resented financial control, and my rebellions kept me broke. The lesson I had to learn was that there is never a freedom that does not have to respect some limitation.

What are the bondages that rob us of important freedoms, and keep us from being who we could be? There are many bondages both internal and external.

Internal bondages are fears, angers, and guilts. We are blocked by all kinds of fears: fear of failure, fear of being found out, fear of illness and death, fear of rejection, fear of loneliness. Our fears are many. They can all be summed up as the fear of others and the fear for ourselves. These fears block us in every effort and gesture. They may imprison us even to the point of suffocation.

Then there are our angers expressed in resentment and hostility. By them we alienate ourselves from others, others from us, and others from each other. Our angers and resentments pollute the world of relationship and our entire spiritual environment. Indeed our angers alienate ourselves from ourselves and God. I have known people whose angers became so obsessive that they saw everything and everybody through their angers and resentment. As such people age they become more and more bitter and resentful. They become so alienated that they lose all capacity for compassion without which a person becomes spiritually dead. What is needed is the spirit that enables us to transmute anger into love.

Then there is guilt. We are vulnerable and egocentric which means that inevitably we will think and do things that we either know or learn are contrary to the goodness of life. We acquire a sense of sin against ourselves, others and the Divine Law. Because of guilt we may despair of our lives and feel that because of our past which we hate we can have no future. As a counselor I have heard many people say: "If I could only wipe out my past, I would feel so free to go on." Our guilts can accumulate and give us a sense of defeat insofar as the quality of our lives is concerned. The bondage of guilt creates in us a sense of worthlessness and lack of integrity as well as a sense of moral possibility.

These are examples—fear, anger, and guilt—of internal bondages that rob us of freedom. And it is for such bondages that St. Paul spoke: "Where the spirit of the Lord is, there is freedom." Is it really possible?

Then there are the external bondages. These are conditions and circumstances over which we have no control: handicaps, accidents that change our resources, events such as war, economic depressions, scandals, failures, and, to use an ancient phrase, "plagues, pestilences and sudden deaths." It is true that to a greater or lesser degree we are victims of our own whims and decisions and outside events and forces. When tragedy strikes one can well ask: Where is any freedom?

What is meant by the spirit of the Lord? Why is it so powerful? And when it works, what happens?

The spirit of the Lord is the spirit of one who faced and accepted the sin and conditions of human life, the same that was just described in ourselves. He allowed himself to be destroyed by them on the cross. He was not defeated; He lived again; He transcended all human bondages. The same spirit in Him is available to us to do the same in relation to our limitations, imprisonments, and tragedies. It is so easy for us to become lost in the shadows of things that befall us. In the Gospel of John we read about the lame man who, for thirty-eight years, remained by the pool of Bethzatha with other invalids waiting for the waters to be troubled and for someone to lift him into the waters so that he could be healed. When Jesus saw him He knew the man had been there for a long time and asked him, "Don't you want to be healed?" The sick man answered Him, "Sir, I have no one to put me into the pool when the water is troubled and another enters and is healed." Then Jesus said to him, "Rise, take up your pallet, and walk." And at once he took up his bed and walked. The spirit of the Lord released powers in the man that enabled him to break the mental and physical bondages of his incapacities. Have we all not had experiences of this kind of release from and freedom for our lives? When we open our minds and hearts to a greater spirit than our own, we discover that we can transcend our former selves.

What is our part in responding to that spirit in order that its powers can heal our bodies and enlarge our souls?

The first step is self-acceptance which means accepting our fears, our guilts, our angers, our incapacities, our circumstances and whatever other bondage we suffer from. It also means accepting our positive powers which we may depreciate or of which we are not aware. The man by the pool had capacities as well as incapacities and like many of us was so much aware of incapacities that he lost awareness of what he could do. Jesus' spirit energized his capacities and he walked. Alcoholic Anonymous provides a good illustration of what acceptance means. There is no hope for cure of alcoholism until there is an acceptance of being alcoholic. We need to accept our weakness, our sickness, and our faults, accept our egocentrism, our defensiveness, our projection of our faults onto others. Acceptance is hard to exercise because we prefer our illusions about ourselves: that we are strong, competent, dependable, and handle things by ourselves. Acceptance means giving up our rationalizations, our excuses and other defensivenesses. Our part in release from bondage is to say, "Yes, I am sick; yes, I need help." When we can honestly say that, suddenly the world looks and feels different. In so doing we have opened the door of our soul and the spirit of the Lord can enter in His own inimitable way and through our friends. We are no longer lonely because we are no longer living defensively against the love and concern of others. And it is a great experience to realize that one is loved in spite of what one is as well as because of what one is, and that realization is possible when one has accepted the whole truth about oneself. In this kind of human relationship I believe that the spirit of the Lord is able to do His miraculous work.

The second step in opening ourselves to the spirit of the Lord is to open our spiritual eyes and look for the more in ourselves and others. Our human tendency is to foreclose on others' possibilities; that is, we use the little that we have learned about them and conclude that that is all the person is. A woman consulted me some time ago about an important decision she had to make. During the conversation I asked her what her husband thought about the matter. She replied with a disparaging shrug of her shoulders, "Oh, him!" On the basis of her experience of him she had foreclosed on the more he might have been to her. We do this to ourselves, too. Because I have negative ways of responding to people, I assume that that is the way I am and have to be, or because I failed I will fail.

Several years ago I had an experience that illustrates what I mean by "looking for the more." My wife and I were visiting an artist-philosopher's studio, and while the two of them were working together I had been given some materials to experiment with. After a while the artist stopped over to see how I was doing. My efforts were disappointing. I said that I wanted to discard what I had done and try again. The artist said, "No, don't throw it away. You can't get rid of the life you have lived; you can only add to it. See what you can do to change the work you have created into something more satisfying." And I did! And that is what you and I have to do in relation to lives we have lived. We are unhappy about and regret a part of them but there they are. We cannot unlive what we are ashamed of. The Lord accepts us as we are and the spirit of the Lord wants us to accept all that we are. What we have lived is us, but there is more in us to be lived, and so we are to seek for and live that more. That is our Lord's faith in us. He believes that with his help we can change our disappointing picture. That is to be my attitude toward myself. Yes, my anger can be transmuted into love, my defensiveness can find a transformed expression of self-acceptance and openness. I can learn to recognize in the tragic experience the spirit's call to selflessness and heroism leading to spiritual growth. This is what is meant by looking for and responding to the more in ourselves.

But we are to look for and encourage the appearance and growth of the more in others, and accept their recognition and encouragement of the more in us. Here is a true concept of the role of parents, teachers, pastors. It is also a true concept of what spiritual growth is. What a wonderful experience it is to be seen for the more that one is. I had my first such experience when I was seventeen years old and was in the midst of a deep depression. My high school principal embodied the spirit of the Lord and freed me from my depression about myself and the decision that I was about to make that would have foreclosed on the possibilities of my life. At a time when I was discouraged about myself he saw and called forth something that I had not realized, namely the creative person that I was capable of being. He made an important contribution not only to my worldly life but to my soul's growth. Spiritual growth does not result from preoccupation with religion per se but from bringing the insights of the spirit to the events, issues and decisions of everyday life.

Great as is the experience of being called forth by the spirit through someone's care, even more exciting is the experience of being the agent of the spirit in seeing and calling forth the more in others so that they can experience the freedom of a higher state of being. People helping people to realize their potentialities and possibilities is the true vocation for human beings. We may think that it is the work of parents, teachers, pastors and therapists, as of course it is, but the spirit of the Lord calls every man and woman to that privilege and blessing. If we could embody such attitudes and action, society would be transformed from an aggregate of competing persons and groups into true community since trust and interdependence would be restored.

As I look back over my life I remember many persons whose sense of spiritual freedom enables them to use their limitations as channels of power for themselves and others: a frail mother living in poverty and pain whose courage, trust and radiant spirit helped me to overcome a tendency to depressions and to face my own problems with more spirit; a dancer who lost her legs in an accident and emerged out of the tragedy with a dancing spirit and a dedication to teaching children to dance and acquire physical and spiritual grace; many men and women who in spite of affliction and loss maintained an equanimity that freed them to see what they had rather than what they had lost. These are the kinds of people who find freedom in spite of limitations, move into the more that is theirs and inspire and encourage the same in others.

This was vividly impressed on me by the example of my mother when I was fifteen years old. We had just moved on to undeveloped land north of Seattle, without roads, and into a cedar shake shack pending the building of a decent home. The next morning a spark from the chimney ignited the roof and in a half hour that tinder dry building was gone with everything we owned. When my father and I returned by trail from the village three miles away with supplies on our backs we found that my mother had prepared a place around a log for lunch. In the middle stood a rusty tin can filled with wild flowers. She was reaching for the more in our situation than on the surface we seemed to have. That can of flowers became a powerful symbol of freedom in the midst of devastating limitations. And we were empowered to re-relate to our desperate situation.

Finally, therefore, a third way in which we can prepare ourselves for the working of the spirit of the Lord is by trying to re-

relate to our world of events and people out of the more we are and with an acceptance of our vulnerability. That is what the artist was asking me to do when she insisted that I keep the messy drawing, get in touch with the more and re-relate to the drawing by adding something that was not there. The change and addition on the inside of us must be manifest in our behavior which is another way of saying that "faith without works is dead."

My pre-teen son and I had an altercation in which I functioned badly. After he stormed out I felt terrible about my role as a father. Shortly after, a couple arrived at my study door for a counseling session. They explained that they needed help in their relationship with their son. I protested that I was in no condition to help them with any problem in that area and explained the reason for my response. But they insisted that I deal with their concern. After an hour or so of discussion they left thanking me for my help. I wondered about how helpful I had been because in the back of my mind was my concern about my son. I discovered, however, that I came out of the session with a sense of more parental resourcefulness than I had had when they arrived. I also found that because of the more I felt in relation to my son I wanted to find him and share with him my sense of failure and also my desire out of a recovered perspective to relate to him and come to a better resolution of our difficulty. So I found him and after a period of strain we finally worked things out.

Our effort to re-relate may not always be that successful, and certainly I have my difficulties in doing it, but it is a necessary step in making ourselves available to the spirit of the Lord who gives us power to break out of the bondage of our fears, angers and guilts.

So let us pray for the insight and desire to admit our vulnerabilities, to look for the more in ourselves and others that is always there, and out of that more to have the courage to readdress ourselves to whatever and whoever needs us while depending on the spirit of the Lord to live with and overcome our limitations.

John 12:24
Isaiah 53:2-4

AGING AND CARING

Henri J. M. Nouwen and Walter J. Gaffney

"Aging and Caring" is a two part sermon series in which Nouwen (see biographical note preceding "Insight and Availability") joins efforts with Walter J. Gaffney. Gaffney is presently administrator for the State Department of Human Resources in Connecticut. He has a background in the social sciences as well as theology and was a teaching assistant for Nouwen at Yale when they collaborated on the book Aging.

The first sermon of the series deals in a wonderfully realistic and affirming way with aging as an aspect of all our lives, the young and the elderly alike, and as a human predicament that can be the way to darkness or to light.

The following sermon on caring can appropriately be termed a classic modern exposition of the meaning of care. It deals first with the person of the carer and the necessity of cultivating such qualities as "poverty" and "compassion." It concludes with the application of this quality of being to the caring situation in terms of acceptance and confrontation, be it the care of the young for the old or vice versa.

I
AGING

Aging is the turning of the wheel, the gradual fulfillment of the life cycle in which receiving matures in giving and living makes dying worthwhile. Aging does not need to be hidden or denied, but can be understood, affirmed, and experienced as a process of growth by which the mystery of life is slowly revealed to us.

Without the presence of old people we might forget that we are aging. The elderly are our prophets; they remind us that what we see so clearly in them is a process in which we all share. Therefore, words about aging may appropriately start with words about the elderly. Their lives are full of warnings but also of hopes.

Much has been written about the elderly, about their physical, mental and spiritual problems, about their need for a good house, good work, and a good friend. Much has been said about the sad situation in which many old people find themselves, and much has been done to try to change this. There is, however, one real danger with this emphasis on the sufferings of the elderly. We might start thinking that becoming old is the same as becoming a problem, that aging is a sad human fate that nobody can escape and should be avoided at all costs, that growing toward the end of the life cycle is a morbid reality that should only be acknowledged when the signs can no longer be denied. Then all our concerns for the elderly become like almsgiving with a guilty conscience, like friendly gestures to the prisoners of our war against aging.

It is not difficult to see that for many people in our world, becoming old is filled with fear and pain. Millions of the elderly are left alone, and the end of their cycle becomes a source of bitterness and despair. There are many reasons for this situation. But underneath all the explanations we can offer, there is the temptation to make aging into the problems of the elderly and to deny our basic human solidarity in this most human process. Maybe we have been trying to silence the voices of those who remind us of our own destiny and have become our sharpest critics by their very presence. Thus our first and most important task is to help the elderly become our teachers again and to restore the broken connections among the generations.

Aging is the most common human experience which overarches the human community as a rainbow of promises. It is an experience so profoundly human that it breaks through the artificial boundaries between childhood and adulthood, and between adulthood and old age. It is so filled with promises that it can lead us to discover more and more of life's treasures. Aging is not a reason for despair but a basis for hope, not a slow decaying but a gradual maturing, not a fate to be undergone but a chance to be embraced.

We therefore hope that those who are old, as well as those who care, will find each other in the common experience of aging, out of which healing and new life can come forth.

An old Balinese legend might help us to think more clearly about our own society and the way we relate to those we have labeled "the old" or "the elderly."

> It is said that once upon a time the people of a remote mountain village used to sacrifice and eat their old men. A day came when there was not a single old man left, and the traditions were lost. They wanted to build a great house for the meetings of the assembly, but when they came to look at the tree-trunks that had been cut for that purpose no one could tell the top from the bottom: if the timber were placed the wrong way up, it would set off a series of disasters. A young man said that if they promised never to eat the old men any more, he would be able to find a solution. They promised. He brought his grandfather, whom he had hidden; and the old man taught the community to tell top from bottom. (Simone de Beauvoir, *The Coming of Age,* New York: C. P. Putman's Sons, 1972, p. 77)

Is it true that in our days we too sacrifice the old, ostracize them and expel them from the community of the living? Have we also lost the traditions which helped us to understand our own lives and now can no longer tell top from bottom?

There indeed is little doubt that for many people growing old is a way to destruction and darkness.

The well-known French author Simone de Beauvoir has published an impressive and well-documented study of aging. After a long and detailed analysis of the biological, ethnological, historical, and phenomenological aspects of aging, she concludes: "The vast majority of mankind looks upon the coming of old age with sorrow or rebellion. It fills them with more aversion than death itself." (*The Coming of Age,* p. 539) Her view of old age seems like a contemporary reflection of the complaint expressed so many years ago in the Thirty-First Psalm. There an old man says:

> Take pity on me, Yahweh, I am in trouble now.
>   Grief wastes away my eye, my throat, my inmost parts.
> For my life is worn out with sorrow, my years with sighs;
>   my strength yields under misery, my bones are wasting away.

I am contemptible, loathsome to my neighbours,
> to my friends a thing of fear.
Those who see me in the street hurry past me;
> I am forgotten, as good as dead in their hearts,
> something discarded. (Psalm 31:9–12, *The Jerusalem Bible*)

We cannot deny these facts and feelings. We even have to enter them and ask ourselves: "What is it that makes many old people feel ostracized?" In light of this question we can note at least three factors: segregation, desolation, and loss of self. We could consider these factors as three forms of rejection: rejection by society, rejection by friends, and rejection by our inner self.

Claire Townsend describes old age as the last segregation. This seems a very appropriate expression in a civilization in which "being" is, in fact, considered less important than "doing" and "having." Our desire to acquire a job, to make a good career, to have a house, a car, money, stocks and bonds, good relations, and a certain amount of knowledge has become so central in our motivation to live that he or she who no longer is able to relate to the world in those "desirable" terms has become a stranger.

Sharon Curtin, a young woman who has worked with the elderly, remarks:

> I have learned that a culture which equates material possessions with success, and views the frantic, compulsive consumer as the perfect citizen, can afford little space for the aged human being. They are past competing, they are out of the game. We live in a culture which endorses what has been called "human obsolescence." After adolescence, obsolescence. To the junk heap, the nursing home, the retirement village, the "Last Resort." (Sharon R. Curtin, *Nobody Ever Died of Old Age,* Boston and Toronto: Little, Brown, and Co., 1972, p. 56)

Although segregation is one of the most important elements in the predicament of the elderly, only a few of them will be consciously aware of its destructive dynamics. In talking about their sadness and sufferings, desolation, not segregation, is uppermost in their minds. Desolation is the crippling experience of the shrinking circle of friends with the devastating awareness that the few years left to live will not allow you to widen the circle again. Desolation is the gnawing feeling of being left behind by those who have been close and dear to you during the many years of life. It is the knowledge of the heart saying that nobody else will be as close to you as the friend you have lost, because a friend is like wine: "When it grows old, you drink it with pleasure." (Sir 9:10 TJB)

Segregation and desolation are powerful factors which create a severe alienation in the elderly. But one way of rejection, which in the final analysis is probably the most destructive, is self-rejection. This is the inner ostracism by which the elderly not only feel they are no longer welcome in the society of profit, or able to keep their small circle of intimate friends together, but by which they also feel stripped of their own feeling of self-worth and are no longer at home in their most inner life. He who has lost his most inner self has nothing left to live for. He can say with Ben Sira in the Old Testament:

O death, your sentence is welcome
    to a man in want, whose strength is failing,
To a man worn out with age, worried about everything,
    disaffected and beyond endurance.

The heavy pessimism pervading Simone de Beauvoir's study, the depressive statistics about the later years of life, and the all-too-visible rejection of the elderly through segregation, desolation, and the loss of self make it indeed difficult to see growing old other than as a way to darkness.

Is this where we have to stop and bow our heads in sadness? We do not believe so, because once in a while a young man might come into our world and tell us that he has hidden the old man who can tell us top from bottom and prevent our assembly house from caving in on us. It is this young man who may unmask the myths about growing old and remind us that aging can indeed also be a way to the light.

Aging As a Way to the Light

We have to say that, in all likelihood, many of the conditions which are the cause of much suffering to the elderly will remain with us for some years to come. But it would be a temptation to allow the darkness to overwhelm us and make us insensitive to the signs of light which become visible in the lives of many old people.

When we are able to cast off our fears and come close to the many who have grown old, we see old men and women telling stories to children with eyes full of wonder and amazement. We think of old Pope John giving life to an old church, and of old Mother Teresa offering hope to the sick and dying in India. We look at the last self-portrait of Rembrandt and discover a depth that was not there before. We marvel at the last works of Michelangelo and realize that they are his best. We remember the strong face of the old Schweitzer, the piercing eyes of the elderly Einstein, and the mild face of Pope Pius X. We recognize the transparency of the farmer looking over his fields in which he has worked for many years, the deep understanding smile of the woman who saw her own children die long before she did, and the concentrated expression on the face of the old poet. We hear people talking about the old country, the olden days, and old friends, as if their pains and joys had composed a melody that is growing to a silent climax. Then we know that slowly but surely, in the broken, beaten faces of the many who belabored the world for years, a new light has become visible—a light that cannot die because it is born out of growing old.

One way of describing the way to the light is to call it a slow conversion from wishes to hope. Wishes have concrete objects such as cars, houses, promotions, and wealth. Hope is open-ended, built on the trust that the other will fulfill his or her promises. When hope grows we slowly see that we are worth not only what we achieve but what we are, that what life might lose in use, it may win in meaning. This is beautifully expressed in an old Taoist parable which tells us about a carpenter and his apprentice who saw a huge oak tree, very old and very gnarled.

> The carpenter said to his apprentice: "Do you know why this tree is so big and so old?"
> The apprentice said: "No . . . why?"
> Then the carpenter answered: "Because it is useless. If it were useful it would have been cut down, sawed up and used for beds and tables and chairs. But, because it is useless, it has been allowed to grow. That is why it is now so great that you can rest in its shadow."

When the value of the tree became the tree itself, it was free to grow to the light. That is the power of hope.

The way to the light is a hopeful way and therefore full of humor. Humor is knowledge with a soft smile. It takes distance but not with cynicism, it relativizes but does not ridicule, it creates space but does not leave you alone. Old people often fill the house with good humor, and make the serious businessman, all caught up in his great projects, sit down and laugh. Knowledge with a soft smile is a great gift. One day an important, highly decorated diplomat knelt down before Pope John, kissed his ring and said: "Thank you, Holy Father, for that beautiful encyclical *Pacem in Terris* which you gave the world." Pope John looked at him with a smile and answered: "Oh, did you read it too?" And when someone asked him: "How many people work in the Vatican?" he thought for a while and then said: "Well, I guess about half of them."

Humor is a great virtue, because it makes you take yourself and your world seriously, but never too much. It brings death into every moment of life, not as a morbid intruder, but as a gentle reminder of the contingency of things.

Hope and humor can give rise to a new vision. Once in a while we meet an old man or woman looking far beyond the boundaries of his or her human existence into a light that seems to embrace him or her with gentleness and kindness. It is a vision that makes them not only detach themselves from preoccupation with the past but also from the importance of the present. It is a vision that invites them to a total, fearless surrender in which the distinction between life and death slowly loses its pain. This vision is most vividly expressed by the Dutch priest Han Fortmann. While traveling in India he discovered that he was suffering from a lethal cancer and had to go home to die. On his deathbed he was able to write, while his strength was slowly fading away, these beautiful words:

> I proceed from the simple irrefutable fact that in the crucial moments of life . . . (such as death), even though people come from diverging cultures and religions, they find that same essential word: Light! For isn't it true? There must be a basic similarity between the Enlightenment spoken of by the Hindus and Buddhists and the Eternal Light of the Christians. Both die into the Light. One practical difference could well be that the Buddhist, more than the contemporary Christian, has learned to live with the light (nirvana) as a reality long before he dies. . . . That interior participation, that Enlightenment, intended "For every man who comes into the world"—as John's gospel put it—has received far less attention in practical preaching than in the teaching of Satori in Zen Buddhism or Samdi in Hinduism. But whoever has once met God no longer finds the hereafter question interesting. Whoever has learned to live in the Great Light is no longer worried by the problem of whether the Light will still be there tomorrow. . . . The need to pose skeptical questions about the hereafter seems to disappear as the divine Light again becomes a reality in everyday life, as it is meant to, of course, in all religions. (Han Fortmann, *Discovery of the East,* Fides Publishers, Inc., 1971, pp. 98–99)

These words, written by a dying man, reveal the nearly overwhelming vision that aging can be a growing into light, the light which takes away all the dark and gray lines that divide religious cultures and people and unites all the colors of the human search into one all-embracing rainbow. It is this vision of the light that may grow in our lives as we are coming of age and may make a narrowing path into a widening avenue.

II
CARING

Is aging a way to the darkness or a way to the light? It is not given to anyone to make a final judgment, since the answer can only be brought forth from the center of our being. No one can decide for anyone else how his or her aging shall be or should be. It belongs to the greatness of men and women that the meaning of their elderly existence escapes the power of calculations and predictions. Ultimately, it can only be discovered and affirmed in the freedom of the heart. There we are able to decide between segregation and unity, between desolation and hope, between loss of self and a new, recreating vision. Everyone will age and die, but this knowledge has no inherent direction. It can be destructive as well as creative, oppressing as well as liberating.

What seems the most frightening period of life, marked by excommunication and rejection, might turn into the most joyful opportunity to tell our community top from bottom. But who is the one who is going to call the elderly from their hiding places? Who is the one who will take their fear away and will lead them out of the darkness of segregation, desolation, and loss of selfhood into the light which is prepared for all the nations to see? Who is that young man who will have the courage to step forward in his society and proclaim that by ostracizing the old men the traditions will be lost and a series of disasters could take place?

It is the one who cares. Through caring, aging can become the way to the light and offer hope *and* new life.

To care one must offer one's own vulnerable self to others as a source of healing. To care for the aging, therefore, means first of all to enter into close contact with your own aging self, to sense your own time, and to experience the movements of your own life cycle. From this aging self, healing can come forth and others can be invited to cast off the paralyzing fear for their future. As long as we think that caring means only being nice and friendly to old people, paying them a visit, bringing them a flower or offering them a ride, we are apt to forget how much more important it is for us to be willing and able to be present to those we care for. And how can we be fully present to the elderly when we are hiding from our own aging? How can we listen to their pains when their stories open wounds in us that we are trying to cover up? How can we offer companionship when we want to keep our own aging self out of the room, and how can we gently touch the vulnerable spots in old people's lives when we have armored our own vulnerable self with fear and blindness? Only as we enter into solidarity with the aging and speak out of common experience can we help others to discover the freedom of old age. By welcoming the elderly into our aging self we can be good hosts and healing can take place. Therefore, when speaking about caring in the context of aging, we want to speak first about caring as the way to the self before we speak about caring as the way to others.

Caring as a Way to the Self

Our first question is not how to go out and help the elderly, but how to allow the elderly to enter into the center of our own lives, how to create the space where they can be heard and listened to from within with careful attention. Quite often our concern to preach, teach, or cure prevents us from perceiving and receiving what those we care for have to offer. Does not healing, first of all, take place by the restoration of a sense of self-worth? But how can that take place unless there is someone able to discover the beauty of the other and willing to receive it as a precious gift? Where else do we realize that we are valuable people except in the eyes of those who by their care affirm our own best self?

Thus care for the elderly means, first of all, to make ourselves available to the experience of becoming old. Only he who has recognized the relativity of his own life can bring a smile to the face of a man who feels the closeness of death. In that sense, caring is first a way to our own aging self, where we can find the healing powers for all those who share in the human condition. No guest will ever feel welcome when his or her host is not at home in his or her own house. No old man or woman will ever feel free to reveal his or her hidden anxieties or deepest desires when they only trigger off uneasy feelings in those who are trying to listen. It is no secret that many of our suggestions, advice, admonitions, and good works are often offered in order to keep distance rather than to allow closeness. When we are primarily concerned with giving old people something to do, offering them entertainment and distractions, we might avoid the painful realization that most people do not want to be distracted but heard, not entertained, but sustained.

Although old people need a lot of very practical help, more significant to them is someone who offers his or her own aging self as the source of their care. What, then, are the characteristics of a caring person, of someone whose care brought him or her in contact with his or her own self? There are obviously many, but two seem most important here: poverty and compassion.

Poverty is the quality of the heart which makes us relate to life, not as property to be defended but as a gift to be shared. Poverty is the constant willingness to say good-bye to yesterday and move forward to new, unknown experiences. Poverty is the inner understanding that the hours, days, weeks, and years do not belong to us but are the gentle reminders of our call to give, not only love and work, but life itself, to those who follow us and will take our place. He or she who cares is invited to be poor, to strip himself or herself from the illusions of ownership and to create some room for the person looking for a place to rest. The paradox of care is that poverty makes a good host. When our hands, heads, and hearts are filled with worries, concerns, and preoccupations, there can hardly be any place left for the stranger to feel at home.

Therefore, to create space for the elderly means, first of all, that I myself must stop relating to my life as to an inalienable property I am obliged to defend at all cost. How can I ever allow the aged to enter into my world when I refuse to perceive my life as a fleeting reality I can enjoy but never grasp, as a precious gift I can foster but never cling to? How can I make any old person feel welcome in my presence when I want to hold on to my life as a possession that nobody can take away from me? How can I create a friendly space for the elderly when I do not want to be reminded of my own historicity and mortality, which make me just as much a "passer-by" as anybody else?

To care for the elderly means then that we allow the elderly to make us poor by inviting us to give up the illusion that we created our own life and that nothing and nobody can take it away from us. This poverty, which is an inner detachment, can make us free to receive the old stranger into our lives and make that person into a most intimate friend.

When care has made us poor by detaching us from the illusion of immortality, we can really become present to the elderly. We can then listen to what they say without worrying about how we answer. We can pay attention to what they have to offer without being concerned about what we can give. We can see what they are in themselves without wondering what we can be for them. When we have emptied ourselves of false occupations and preoccupations, we can offer free space to old strangers, where not only bread and wine but also the story of life can be shared.

In a poor heart compassion can grow, because in a poor heart the pains of growing old can be recognized and shared. Compassion is the second most important characteristic of caring since it allows us to overcome the fear of old strangers and invite them as guests into the center of our own intimacy. When we have taken away the artificial and often defensive distinctions between young and old, we will be able to share the common burdens of aging. Then those who care and those who are cared for no longer have to relate to each other as the strong to the weak, but both can grow in their capacity to be human.

Compassion makes us see beauty in the midst of misery, hope in the center of pain. It makes us discover flowers between barbed wire and a soft spot in a frozen field. Compassion makes us notice the balding head and the decaying teeth, feel the weakening handgrip and the wrinkling skin, and sense the fading memories and slipping thoughts, not as a proof of the absurdity of life, but as a gentle reminder that "unless a wheat grain falls on the ground and dies, it remains only a single grain, but if it dies, it yields a rich harvest." (John 12:24 TJB) Compassion makes us break through the distance of pity and bring our human vulnerability into a healing closeness to our aging brother and sister. Compassion does not take away the pains and agonies of growing old, but offers the place where weaknesses can be transformed into strengths. Compassion heals because it brings us together in patience, that is, in a purifying waiting for the fulfillment of our lives.

Caring as a Way to the Other

Caring can lead to a new self-understanding, but this self-understanding can never be its own goal. We are for others. Therefore we are called to put our aging self at the service of the aging other. The challenge of care for the elderly is that we are called to make our own aging self the main instrument of our healing.

It seems important, however, to say that caring for the aging is not a special type of care. As soon as we start thinking about care for the aging as a subject of specialization, we are falling into the trap of societal segregation, which care is precisely trying to overcome. Caring for the aged asks for a life style in which the generations are brought into contact with each other in a creative way. Those who are in touch with their own aging self might be able to offer the ground where grandfathers and grandmothers, fathers and mothers, sons and daughters, grandsons and granddaughters can come and work together to bring forth the fruits of the earth which are given to them.

Having stressed that caring for the aging other is not a special type of care, we would now like to describe the two main characteristics of caring as the way to others: acceptance and confrontation.

What does caring mean when we think of the many people for whom growing old has become a way to the darkness? What is there to say to men and women who feel forgotten and lonely and who are approaching death as the only way to escape their misery? How do we listen when there are no words of joyous memories, happy events, and a growing light? How do we respond to those who feel that all their fears, but none of their hopes, have been fulfilled?

There are no easy answers to these questions. There does not seem to be a right reaction or response that fits the occasion. The mystery of a failing life is too deep to grasp. But perhaps, while looking into the tired and despairing eyes of the elderly, we might see what Isaiah saw:

> Without beauty, without majesty (we saw him),
> no looks to attract our eyes;

a thing despised and rejected by men,
a man of sorrows and familiar with suffering,
a man to make people screen their faces;
he was despised and we took no account of him.
And yet ours were the sufferings he bore,
ours the sorrows he carried. (Isaiah 53:2–4 TJB)

The painful suffering of many old people which makes their aging into a way of darkness cannot be understood by pointing to their mistakes, weaknesses, or sins. By doing so we might avoid the realization that the fate of many old people reflects an evil that is the evil of a society in which love has been overruled by power, and generosity by competition. They are not just suffering for themselves but for all of us who are, knowingly or unknowingly, responsible for their condition.

It is in the honest and painful recognition of human rejection that God's acceptance can be affirmed. It does not make sense to point to little consoling events in the past which can be held on to. It does not make sense to say: "Yes, I see you are miserable, but look at your happy children, the people you helped and the things you left behind." That only increases guilt feelings and denies the reality of the experience of failure. The only hope is in the simple fact that someone who dares to listen and to face the failing life in its naked reality will not run away but say with a word, a touch, a smile or friendly silence: "I know—you had only one life to live and it cannot be lived again, but I am here with you and I care." Maybe in the midst of this darkness, God's acceptance can be felt through the gentle touch of the one who cares and allows the miserable stranger into his own home.

Acceptance is crucial for many elderly people, but it should not be understood as a passive agreement with the facts of life. On the contrary, care is more than helping people accept their fate. Real care includes confrontation. Care for the aging, after all, means care for all ages, since all human beings—whether they are ten, thirty, fifty, seventy, or eighty years old—are participating in the same process of aging. Therefore, care for the aging means, more often than not, confronting all men and women with their illusion of immortality out of which the rejection of old age comes forth.

It is indeed the task of everyone who cares to prevent people—young, middle-aged, and old—from clinging to false expectations and from building their lives on false suppositions. If it is true that people age the way they live, our first task to to help people discover life styles in which "being" is not identified with "having," self-esteem does not depend on success, and goodness is not the same as popularity. Care for the aging means a persistent refusal to attach any kind of ultimate significance to grades, degrees, positions, promotions, or rewards, and the courageous effort to keep men and women in contact with their inner self, where they can experience their own solitude and silence as potential recipients of the light. When one has not discovered and experienced the light that is love, peace, forgiveness, gentleness, kindness, and deep joy in the early years, how can one expect to recognize it in old age? As the Book of Sirach says: "If you have gathered nothing in your youth, how can you find anything in your old age?" (Sirach 25:3–4, TJB) That is true not only of money and material goods, but also of peace and purity of heart.

Confrontation, by which room is created to allow the eternal light to break into the darkness, is the radical side of care, because it promotes a risky detachment from the concerns of the world and a free manifestation of that love which can change the shape of our society. It not only unmasks the illusions but also makes visible the healing light that gives us the "power to become children of God."

We want to conclude with a story about a painter, Asher Lev, a young Jewish boy from Brooklyn who experienced acceptance and confrontation in the words of his caring father.

In Chaim Potok's book *My Name Is Asher Lev,* this young painter says about himself:

> I drew . . . the way my father looked at a bird lying on its side
> against the curb near our house.
> "Is it dead, Papa?" I was six and could not bring myself to
> look at it.
> "Yes," I heard him say in a sad and distant way.

"Why did it die?"

"Everything that lives must die."

"Everything?"

"Yes."

"You too Papa? And Mama?"

"Yes."

"And me?"

"Yes," he said. Then he added in Yiddish, "But may it be only after you live a long and good life, my Asher."

I could not grasp it. I forced myself to look at the bird. Everything alive would one day be as still as that bird?

"Why?" I asked.

"That's the way the Ribbono Shel Olom made his world, Asher."

"Why?" I asked.

"So life would be precious, Asher. Something that is yours forever is never precious!"

The care of the old for the young is no different from the care of the young for the old. Real care takes place when we are no longer separated by the walls of fear, but have found each other on the common ground of the human condition, which is mortal but, therefore, very, very precious.

CELEBRATION IN THE DESERT

1 Corinthians 3:1–6
Hosea 2:16–17, 21–22
Mark 2:18–22

Father John P. Zenz

Father John P. Zenz has a background in philosophy, theology and spirituality, and at the time of writing was working on his dissertation for an S.T.D. in spirituality from the Gregorian University in Rome. His experience as a parish priest was combined with part-time teaching and retreat conducting responsibilities. As of June 1981 he was assigned as Head of the Theology Department and Dean of Students of Sacred Heart Seminary College in Detroit.

His homily *Celebration in the Desert* was addressed to patients in the cancer ward of Carlo Forlanini Hospital in Rome, Italy on the Sunday immediately preceding the beginning of Lent. It is a beautiful example of interweaving the message of the day's lessons with the realities of the hearer's situation. It underscores the central tenet of the New Testament that we celebrate Jesus as Emmanuel, God-with-us, in the depths as well as the heights of life.

This week the Lenten season begins. Thoughts of Lent bring many different memories and reactions. For some of us, it is a time of special penance. For others, it is a time of promise and hope because it means that Easter (and presumably spring!) is only a few short weeks away.

Maybe many of you are like me. I remember dreading the approach of Lent because it meant no candy, no ice cream, no dessert. It meant going to church for Stations of the Cross. It seemed as if it was a season of endurance. I remember wanting only one thing: I wanted Lent to finally end. I wanted to escape, to be free, to do what I wanted to do and to eat whatever I wanted to eat whenever I wanted to eat it.

We all have memories of days when we tried to run away, to escape, and we all know now as adults that in many ways there is no escape.

In fact, you know that much better than I. Each week I come here for Mass with you; we visit and pray. But I leave. I walk away, even at times eagerly, for the pain of sharing in your suffering can at times be too demanding. I walk away. But you cannot. You stay here, often all alone with your pain, and no one or nowhere to turn. You live in the desert—even here in the midst of a noisy crowded hospital, lying in the aisleways on your stretchers, barely able to catch a glimpse of the sun or to feel a hint of the spring breezes already in the air.

As we prepare to "celebrate" (and that *is* the right word, the "new" word for) this season of Lent, I struggle with what penance I should pursue to remind me of the Lord's presence, to beg forgiveness for my sins, and to pledge my desire to grow in love. But then I think of you who *live* with the Lord in the desert (Hosea reading). I go searching for the desert. I go searching, hoping that the desert will be brief and that I can go back to my desserts. But you are already there. You are in the desert because the Lord has called you and "espoused you forever." In many ways, I realize that I am not worthy to speak to you, for it is rather *you* who give the homily to me. By your patient endurance, by your humble trust, by your persistent and relentless smiles, you teach me. You remind me and so many others that we cannot run away, that we must learn to care but also not to care—for ourselves, for our petty worries and fears. How true the words of Paul to the Corinthians this morning: "You are my letter.... Clearly you are a letter of Christ ... written not with ink but by the Spirit of the living God, not on tablets of stone but on tablets of flesh in the heart."

Yes, you inspire me and challenge me to deeper faith. The Lord is with you, and you are his instruments. And yet, very rightly, you might raise the question: Well and fine, padre. All that is beautiful and easy to say. By our sickness, others are reminded of God's presence and their good fortune. But why not some other way? Why not let us be signs of God's *healing* and miracles? Why must we stay?

Your question is so fair, so just. In fact it is so much like the very question of the gospel today, or, better, the question behind the question: Why do your disciples not fast? Why do some cel-

ebrate the wedding feast and others suffer? Why do I so often feel
that I am alone in this desert? You say, padre, that in the desert
and darkness we will find the light of faith and the Lord. But why
does the desert and this pain leave me feeling still more doubts?

I, too, search for answers. All of us do—whether we are in the
very clearly defined desert of this hospital, living on borrowed
time, or whether we live in the more elusive and more encom-
passing desert of the busy streets and flashing neon lights and
signs of the city.

What comes to mind is a passage of Graham Greene, from
his novel *Monsignor Quixote*. Padre Quixote is traveling through
Spain, trying to convince the communist mayor of his little village
that he should believe in the Lord. The more he tries to argue
with him about the need for faith, the more Father Quixote feels
alien from faith himself.

> Sleep continued to escape him, while the terrible dream of his
> siesta stayed with him like a cheap tune in his head. He had
> dreamt that Christ had been saved from the Cross by the
> legion of angels to which on an earlier occasion the Devil had
> told Him that He could appeal. So there was no final agony,
> no heavy stone which had to be rolled away, no discovery of
> an empty tomb. Father Quixote stood there watching on Gol-
> gotha as Christ stepped down from the Cross triumphant and
> acclaimed. The Roman soldiers, even the Centurion, knelt in
> His honor, and the people of Jerusalem poured up the hill to
> worship Him. The disciples clustered happily around. His
> mother smiled through her tears of joy. There was no ambi-
> guity, no room for doubt and no room for faith at all. The
> whole world knew with certainty that Christ was the Son of
> God.

> It was only a dream, of course, it was only a dream, but none-
> theless Father Quixote had felt on waking the chill of despair
> felt by a man who realizes suddenly that he has taken up a
> profession which is of use to no one, who must continue to live
> in a kind of Saharan desert without doubt or faith, where
> everyone is certain that the same belief is true. He found him-

self whispering, "God save me from such a belief." (Graham Greene, *Monsignor Quixote*, New York: Simon and Schuster, 1982, pp. 69–70)

Lord, save us from thinking we have all the answers. Help us to live in the desert with the questions. Thank You for moments of light that enable us to endure days of darkness.

So often our faith is not really faith. We are like the people Jesus describes in His parable in today's gospel. We use faith like a patch, a band-aid to cover our sores. We try to "scissor and paste" our way through life with a little bit of prayer, but I guess that that is not faith. That is as foolish as new wine in old skins. It is too painful, too risky to throw out old skins, old habits, old ways of looking at life and myself and what's important.

But that is exactly what happens in sickness. The Lord reminds us that "losing our skin," being sick, wasting away on the outside is part of an inner renewal and rebirth. We must all realize—whether we are physically ill or physically strong—that we are all torn and patches *won't* do.

That's what the gospel controversy from Mark's passage for this morning is all about. Jesus is explaining that just external fasting is not enough; it's like a patch sewn on old clothes. Maybe that was what was wrong with our "old" Lent, the Lent when we did so many penitential things and tried to "grin and bear it." We were just scratching the surface and not really changing our lives and ways of doing things. In fact, maybe our very penances became one more thing to *do* to "earn" forgiveness, to "prove" our worth; maybe they became escapes from the *real* desert.

Why do *we* fast? For some of us, just as in Jesus' day, it is a matter of an annual routine. For others, it is a convenient motivation for that postponed diet. If that is the case, I'm sure that our fast will always be too slow, too unnecessarily painful and meaningless.

What should we do for Lent, then? What should we *do*? Maybe we ask the wrong question. Maybe it should be, "What is the *Lord* doing *for me* this Lent?" What challenge, what suffering, what desert is He helping me with this season? What physical pain? What loneliness? What troublesome, complaining neighbor? What forgetful and too-busy friend who disappoints me with lack of love and sympathy?

I remember when I was a child that I used to *look for* penances for Lent—something qualified, not too demanding or involved, and yet no matter how small, it seemed too large. Maybe now I understand that the "groom is with us" as Jesus explains in the gospel. The Lord is near and loves us. I don't need to look for penances; they are already here—in my pain, in *your* pain. Lent means accepting the Lord's nearness to us today. Lent means not running away. Lent means sitting still in this desert, being in the only source of lasting peace—that I am loved, and that it is the Lord who is with me in this desert place, these other people and their needs and pains. And so we prepare, then, not so much for this coming Easter in six weeks, but for an eternal Easter and a heavenly spring.

EXPERIENCING DEATH:
THE CHURCH THEN AND NOW

Father Diarmuid McGann

Born, reared, educated, and ordained in Ireland, Father Diarmuid McGann has spent the last seventeen years in parish work and is currently assistant pastor of the Parish of St. Patrick in Bayshore, N.Y. While in the United States he has studied at and received advanced degrees in Divinity, Pastoral Counseling, and Spiritual Direction from the American Foundation of Religion and Psychiatry, Immaculate Conception Seminary, Iona College, and the Office for Spiritual Direction, Archdiocese of New York. He is the author of a number of poems, six of which have been adapted for TV in a program entitled "Innervision." He was also a consultant on the thirteen part TV series on marriage commissioned by the United States Catholic Conference.

The sermon *Experiencing Death: The Church Then and Now* was given on the occasion of the death of a young girl, Debbie Petrocelli, who died one night of an asthma attack in her father's car on the way to the hospital. She had been a member of McGann's parish and he had been part of her adolescent search for identity. In the sermon McGann masterfully relates the experience of the grieving congregation to that of the grieving church following Jesus' crucifixion. The effect is for the particular contemporary grief to be lifted into a higher unity with the universal experience of the church throughout history, for comfort to flow from a common affirmation of feeling and faith, memory and mystery, without in any way denying or discounting the present reality.

I have picked this passage today to reflect on because it is the story of the church at the moment of the death of Jesus. On that day there were only two of them on the road but they were truly his church. Now we are the church. We are gathered at Debbie's death. We are considerably more in number but the experience we share is similar to theirs. I would like to use four words to describe the experience of the church on that day, and they are the same four words I would use to describe our experience today.

First I see them as a church of feeling. The scripture says they were walking the road. They were going from Jerusalem, a place of peace, to a place somewhere in the distance. They were going from the known to the unknown. As they went on that journey they "were talking together." They were "discussing the events of the past few days." Their faces were "sad and downcast." They are described as men who are trying to get a hold on their experience. Something has happened and they are shocked and the whole thing doesn't fit together. The other gospel stories tell us even more. Thomas for instance is described as being isolated, alone. He is not with Mary, not with the apostles, not in the upper room. He doesn't believe the story he hears from the others and he won't accept anything from Jesus except concrete evidence. Thomas' response to Jesus' death sounds like anger. He won't need anyone again. Mary Magdalene by contrast is in the cemetery when she meets a gardener. She doesn't recognize him, for when he asks her what she is doing there she says, "They have taken away my Lord and I don't know where they have put him." Her response sounds as though she feels more than anything else the absence of Jesus. The one she loved is gone. That's what she knows; that's all she knows. Peter too has his own feelings and the scripture paints him as having gone back to fishing, to doing what he was doing before he ever met Jesus. Peter regressed to a former style of existence, and significantly enough the scripture says that though he worked all night he caught nothing.

We too are a church of feeling. With Debbie's death we are thrown into many responses. Sometimes it all seems so very real; sometimes it seems like a dream. We are bounced around inside until at times we feel like a tennis ball. Each of us has had our own individual response, our own feeling about her death, and we spend these moments discussing all that's happened in the past few days. Some of us are feeling the shock of her death, a kind of numbness; others are feeling a great anger. Maybe it's an unfocused anger, or maybe it's very focused and we are angry at God for taking her, or angry at her for dying. The experience of others right now is different. All they know and feel is that Debbie is gone, that she is dead. Others are wondering if perhaps they did something different, or if they said something else, or if this or that didn't happen would she have died. We like the early church on the road to Emmaus are a church of feeling.

Secondly, they were a church of faith. They were walking the road when Jesus came and walked with them, but they didn't recognize him. However he is the topic of their conversation. They were discussing his presence among them, his absence, and now their future. One of them puts it succinctly when he says, "We were hoping that he was the one who would set Israel free." They are seeing how once they had it all together and now they don't. In John's gospel, at the Last Supper Jesus announces his departure, and the response of those present is, "What is he talking about?" "What does he mean?" "What is the little while?" (John 16:16ff) They are brought to a new questing. What does it mean now to live in the Spirit of God? Who is God now? What is the face of Jesus like now in the light of this experience? Jesus himself speaks in Matthew's gospel of God as Father, but when he comes to Gethsemane he experiences the other side of that image of God. There he experiences that God is not like a Father. He allows his Son to undergo the temptation and the testing, and in Matthew's gospel Jesus dies not with the word "Father" on his lips, but with the words "My God, my God." He is brought by life and its experience to redefine who God is and who he is.

We are a church of faith. Now we are going through an experience when perhaps our familiar experience of God is being eclipsed and we do not know or recognize the face of God that we see. It's the face of a stranger, it's different, it's not what we expected. We have been brought by Debbie's death to a garden where God is unfamiliar and in the light of tragedy we are forced to ask new questions. Sitting in the funeral home, sitting in the church today, sitting at home in the evening in these past few days became painful and yet comforting as the questions come into our hearts whether we like it or not—questions that ask the meaning of Debbie's life and death, of our life and death: What now is the face of God? What does it mean now to say God is love?

What does it mean now for us to believe? Yet in the middle of that it is the face of God we seek. We are a people of faith.

As I return to the story of Emmaus, the third word that seems to describe the church for me is to say they are a church of memory. When Jesus joins them and enters into their pain, he brings them back to their tradition; he returns with them to the scriptures and explains to them "all those passages which referred to him." He remembers with them the story of God involving himself in human history. In the first part of the story they do all the talking. They are, however, gradually brought into silence, and it's only when they have talked out their feelings and despair and discouragement that his time comes to talk and he enables them to remember what they had forgotten. He extends their limited memory into the limitless memory of God so that their loss and their pain and their suffering is seen as part of Jesus' suffering and pain. It was necessary for the Messiah to suffer and then to enter his glory.

We too are a church of memory. Everyone here has a special memory of Debbie. Her Mom and Dad, brothers and sisters have very special memories. Some are thinking of her birth, her growing years, her school, etc. Yesterday I was sharing some of those memories with you and with her family at the funeral home. Each of us has a personal memory whether that of teacher, friend, uncle, aunt, etc. A favored image I'm sure is returning to your mind even as I speak. My own memory is of Debbie with a smile on her face, shyly half turned from me yet very aware of everything that was going on. I see her now sitting in my office sharing with me her hopes and goals for the future. But today I want to share a larger memory than that with you. I know something essential about Debbie. She was baptized in the life of Jesus and anointed in this church in the Spirit of Jesus; she followed in this parish the way of Jesus, and signed herself publicly among us with the cross of Jesus. You cannot, therefore, say who Debbie is apart from saying who Jesus is, for she chose to identify her life with his. Who was Jesus but the presence among us of the goodness and love of God? Who is Debbie but another touch of God's goodness? Someone we could, to use John's description of Jesus, have heard, and seen with our own eyes, someone we have looked upon and our hands have touched, a word of life.

The last word I would leave with you is to say they were a church of mystery. They came in the evening to a little village and it looked as though Jesus would go on, but they asked him to come in with them and they gathered around a table. It was a strange table. So much of their life with him was centered at a table, whether he was the host or they were. It was a place they liked to be together. But the table was for them a paradox. On the one hand it is the table of the Last Supper, of his going away from them. On the other hand it is the table of the Eucharist at which he can be with them forever. On the one hand it is the table of sacrifice and pain as he went from the table to Calvary. On the other hand it is the table of life and love where he can share with them his own presence. On the one hand it is the table of his loneliness as he faces the certainty of his own destiny. On the other hand it is the table of community where he meets his people. On the one hand it is the table of absence. On the other hand, it is the table of presence. It is in short the table of mystery where Jesus as problem to be solved becomes forever Jesus as life to be lived.

We too are a church of mystery gathered now around another altar table. It is for us a paradox too; it is the table at which we say goodbye to Debbie as she goes from us into death. It is also the table at which we can meet her each day because of our belief that the church on earth and in heaven is one. It is the table that speaks of her pain and suffering and ours, but it is also the table that speaks of our life and love for her and hers for us. It is the table at which we can remember destiny in a short but full life and also remember ours.

So we are here as a church of feeling and faith, a church of memory and mystery. The last thing mentioned in the story of Emmaus is that this group of disciples returned to Jerusalem and found the eleven and shared with them their story "of what happened on the road." As they did this, they became for Luke, in the middle of their own brokenness and pain, the new witnesses to the resurrection. So too are we. For a long time we will need to talk about what happened on the road, of what happened to us when Debbie died. We will need to join the eleven, the other members of the church, and listen to their story. We need to take a walk with one another again and see how once we thought we had it all together, but now the bottom has fallen out of our lives. We need to pray again with a lot of feeling and talking and discouragement, and then maybe we too will arrive at a place where he will speak, where he will talk, where he will reveal to us the meaning of this suffering and pain. We are like the man that Eliot describes in his poem "Four Quartets." We now are in the darkness. What do you do in the darkness? we ask, and Eliot responds:

> I said to my soul, be still and wait
> Without hope, for hope would be hope for the wrong thing
> Wait without love, for love would be love of the wrong thing
> There is yet faith, but the faith, and the hope
> And the love are all in the waiting
> Wait without thought for you are not ready for thought
> Yet to the darkness shall be the light, and the stillness the
> dancing.

We too are waiting, not knowing what to think, whom to love, what to hope for, and yet we believe. We wait in the darkness, in the silence, in this moment that time is, until he speaks and makes all things new.

John 16:31–33
Isaiah 53

PASSIONS OF
THE MIND: GRIEF

Robert L. Benefiel

Robert L. Benefiel was one of the early pastors to enter into an intensive period of clinical pastoral training and to carry the spirit and insight of that experience through a lifetime career in parish ministry. During his period of clinical training Benefiel was exposed to the early work on grief being conducted by Rabbi Joshua Liebman.

He deals with the reality of grief in this wide ranging sermon titled *Passions of the Mind: Grief.* The sources of personal and social grief, typical reactions to grief, the general cycle that grief processes go through as well as implications for the individual and greater community for dealing with grief are all discussed and richly illustrated. (The sermon assumes an overall perspective on grief that molds the distinction Wayne Oates would make between anticipatory and acute grief.)

We have saved the most delicate and the most difficult, even dangerous, sermon in this series on "inner passions" to the end. There is considerable freedom speaking about fear, loneliness, and guilt, for these are fairly common everyday experiences which we can share with each other in a rather frank manner. But when we come to grief, it can be such a private, intimate, and devastating monster that many times we can share our grief with only one, and sometimes no one but God.

It is however one passion which every mortal has sometime during his or her life, and for some life can become unending grief. The greats in their chateaus as well as the solitary peasants in their grass-thatched shacks may have their souls literally blasted apart by grief. The rich and the poor, the wise and the ignorant, the holiest saints and most miserable sinners all suffer alike when there is a great loss, bitter disappointment, aching discouragement, or soulful regret. It is our best friends as well as our worst enemies that come to times when their souls are ripped by sadness and sorrow, and sometimes are infected for life. Here is an experience that testifies to the universal commonality of humankind.

Our personal grief comes from *two principal sources.* (1) The first is the loss of someone dear or something significant which decimates our life by its absence. (2) The second source comes from the loss of faith, confidence, and ideals. Actually, grief is such a global experience at times that whatever source it began with, it reaches to the other realm as well. Loved ones die, move away, are committed to hospitals and rest homes by our own reluctant hands. Our business or profession is somehow wrenched from us for whatever reasons. Our book is rejected because of marketing conditions, and we sense that our faith, trust, and confidence, those things which undergird all our particular activities, are somehow ebbing and not providing us with the energy and motivation we once had. Ruthless floods, tornadoes, and volcanic eruptions such as Mount St. Helen's in our own backyard come and wipe out human beings and property as though they were weeds in a field, and then we can wonder, wonder how to put one foot in front of the other with such a gnawing sense of emptiness and hopelessness. Physical diseases and mental illness plague individuals and reduce their days to tragic cycles of meaninglessness.

In the last fifteen years we have been especially affected by the loss of faith and ideals that comes from grief associated with radical change. Our self-concept as a people has been severely rattled as we have begun to realize that the world does not look upon us as the model of freedom and decency and benevolent power we once thought. Our might and resources were not able to carry the day in a small Asian country. We were certainly not even thanked for our effort, and our foreign policy is continually under suspicion as some critics point to the support of totalitarian regimes for the sake of profit alone. Our young men and women, the product of the best environment we could conceive, came back to us from Vietnam with severe, scrambled, decimated identities from being under intense pressure and anxiety not knowing who the enemy was, not knowing if they were being good or bad signing up in the first place, not being welcomed wholeheartedly back into the mainstream of American life once they returned. The barbarity of human nastiness and the awesomeness of man's inhumanity to man, that many of us are shielded from in suburban life, has come through to us in a sickening way as the tactics and effects of multinational corporations have been revealed bit by bit; revelations that show the ill effects on the health development of other countries without anybody in particular to point at as being guilty or responsible; simply thousands of people going to work every day, trying to do a good job with the best intentions, and finding after the fact that perhaps they are manufacturing carcinogens, vicious weapons of chemical warfare, food devoid of nourishment, are developing medical procedures that complicate as much as heal, are using materials that make a country's economy one product dependent instead of a diversified feeder of itself, and on and on.

People can actually become paralyzed by the shattering of their dreams. In the story of the Jews in the Old Testament, when they were conquered and carried off into strange lands and cultures, away from their identity and worship in relation to the temple, there are records of many dying literally from grief, each time. When I first began my ministry many of the oldtimers thought of "going to the hospital to have a baby" as something alien and equated being put in convalescent homes with wicked connotations. And sure enough, all of our pride in modern science, gadgets, and methods to the contrary, we are seeing that the more depersonalized and mechanized our society becomes, the more we are paying the price in apathy, violence and senseless deaths. Even when we tear down slums and ghettos with wonderful intentions to pave the way for more modernized high rise housing, high death rates are predictable.

And so there are the subtle and not easy to pin down reverberations throughout the culture, partly associated with grief, with dropping out, doping up, not respecting authority or property, not rallying to any concrete cause or purpose, not having prisons enough or policemen enough to patrol a society not bound together with the internalized glue of common hopes, faith, values and aspirations.

Particular *reactions to grief,* from whatever sources, will of course be varied and individual with no two people ever experiencing it the same way. For full blown grief however, we can paint some broad brush strokes that have predictability. From little children to toddering old age, we can be aware that the following are common. (1) Grief leaves us shocked, numbed, confused, and often unbalanced. (2) We lose interest not only in ourselves but also in the outside world. (3) Our desire for normal human experiences, interests, affections, and enthusiasms may be diluted. (4) Strange, out-of-character sensations such as anger or cynicism may take over that we experience negatively. (5) As loneliness grows, depression can be triggered and with it guilt, futility, fatigue and anti-social attitudes.

The Christian faith cannot stop tragedies from coming, so far as I know, or the natural consequences associated with the loss of what we have invested our heart and soul in. It can help color our understanding of what is going on and channel us in the direction of God's healing and grace. If our own prayers and efforts as well as those of the healing community that surrounds us are to be pertinent, we need, it seems to me, some notion of the devastating human event, all the while knowing it is *one event,* a *process* with a beginning, middle, and end, a healing *cycle* that does not last forever. The stages of the cycle of grief have been delineated as *shock, mourning, and recovery.* Let us look at how Christian faith and love minister to grief-stricken persons as they move through these powerful periods of human existence. Our conviction is that each of these developments lies within the reach of God and God's children, and that none of us need feel abandoned when the teeth of tragedy rip into our beings. Out of his deep spiritual intuition, Isaiah was right when he said: "Surely he hath born our griefs, and carried our sorrow." There are definite resources for continuity, healing, and even greater growth throughout the grieving process.

It is normal to be shocked when some tragedy breaks up the unity of a family, a relationship, or a life's course. It is normal for the shock to manifest itself in feelings of isolation, restlessness, helplessness, and hopelessness.

In this situation it is important that our prayer life become enlivened on our own behalf. "O God, strengthen my desire for deliverance." "Help me not to be consumed by this temporary condition." "Help me to tap my healing resources." We might also need to pray sometimes, "God, give me the passion to pray at all." "Lord, say for me the sighs that are too deep for words." If we find we can't even bring ourselves to pray at all, we probably need to look closely at our negativity and take inspiration from one like Tevye in "Fiddler on the Roof" who can help us know that we can pray any prayer that comes with integrity from within. That would definitely include such psalmistic cries as, "Why me, O God? Why now? How can I go on? What am I to do?"

And sometimes our prayer needs to be: "O God, help me to deal realistically with my grief, and to ignore the trivial and superficial advice of well-meaning but unwise persons." A young widow once confessed:

> Everyone told me I must not cry in front of my six-year-old daughter. It would leave such emotional scars. I took the advice. Then, one day, she asked me: "You're glad Daddy died, aren't you, Mommy? Why didn't you love Daddy?" Believe me, after we'd cried together, things were a lot easier for both of us. You can't fool children—why try?

Our first job in the midst of shock and grief is to know who we are, what we are experiencing, *to be who we are* and to trust that that is where the God of a good creation will meet us. Putting on any kind of phony act is a dangerous life-strategy, especially in the crisis-time of life with grief.

Many people in our culture definitely do feel called upon to deny the existence and the worth of so called negative emotions as a valid component of life. This is self-defeating because life has explosive energies, labeled both positive and negative, and both function. This case-history is illustrative:

> A grieving widow had picked up the notion that she should "put up a brave front, and face life with a smile." An ingenious and strong person, she recovered sufficiently to get a job and have some social life—but she was depressed. She had deeply adored her husband, but one night, after eighteen months of widowhood, she found herself staring angrily at his picture. Spontaneously, she began to shout: "Why did you do

this to me? How could you leave me alone like this?" In blind
fury, she snatched the picture off the dresser and slammed it
to the floor screaming, "Damn you! Damn you! Damn you!"

The next day she went to see her doctor and fortunately he
supported her experience and explained: "In your mind, you
know your husband didn't die to punish you. But when he
died, you did feel abandoned. This is a normal human reaction. Finally you've made contact with your honest feelings.
Now let's talk about what else you feel."

With careful assistance, this lady discovered that her life-
strategy was to repress all her negative thoughts and feelings—anger, hostility, guilt, self-pity—because *they made
her feel wrong!* After she had gained a wholesome realistic
understanding she sighed and said: "How can a person spend
so long a time hiding from herself?'

How many people around about us believe that they can
solve dollar-sized problems with nickle techniques? "O God, help
me to use all of me that you have given me in facing my grief."

The role of the community in ministering to shock is obviously to be there in the midst of it. To incarnate love is not to
cover up shock in any way but to help be a shock absorber. We
support people by our presence, by our courage in not running
from the reality we find, by our living affirmation of the inherent
self-regulating, self-directing, self-healing processes we possess.
God has given us this wonderful, awesome, built-in capacity for
sores to heal, bones to mend, appetites to return. Certainly we
provide affirmation of the worth of the person to us, regardless of
the loss of their spouse, job, scholarship, physical appendage, girl
friend, car, or whatever. The community in general, provides sta-
bilizing experiences, and it encourages Christian attitudes—to be
kind to the self, to be forgiving of the event.

The period of mourning is a time of accommodation to hurt,
pain, and anguish over this huge chunk of existence taken away
from us. It is a time to pray for patience and tolerance with the
need for *time* to do its work, to make changes and adjustments.

It is a time for the griever and the community to join in encouraging a rejoining of the human race, however many imperfect and insensitive mortals there are cluttering up the universe. And it is a time for an acceptance of all that we have felt, and will feel, as a natural, necessary part of dealing with grief. Grief, like worship, can be viewed as a liturgy, a work and service that we carry out and live through on behalf of ourselves, the community, and God.

Grief does tend to arouse dormant forces within all of us, whose presence are detriments to ourselves and others. If you sense you're not making progress, there is the need to express your suffering as noted above or in some way to investigate what might be holding you back. Grief is a natural healing process. It grabs us and shakes us in the heart and guts of our being if we allow it to have its way, but there is the unmistakable inner confirmation that it is healing us. If we don't seem to have this growing realization over time, we need to focus on the impediments of the process: in quietness we can look inside and see if what seems to bubble up from our diffuse overall sense of ourselves is fear of the future, anger, guilt, self-pity, blame, holding on to hostility, or whatever. Noting it, acknowledging it, naming it, and letting it have its reality will tend to shift it and pave the way for continued growth.

If none of this works, it is serious not to seek help in time. Grief is not something the human organism can cope with unaided: Grief has to do with the loss of some kind of relationship—either a human one or one that gets its juice vicariously from a human one. It is a natural urge to avoid suffering and to seek the supposed peace of death rather than to struggle with life. We often need the grace of another, someone beyond ourselves, to help us transcend our despair. No one *wishes* to tangle with grief, not even our Lord: "O Father, if it be thy will let this cup pass from me." And remember how he went looking for company to stand by him and was disappointed to the core to find his friends sleeping and unable to share his tribulation. Listen now to this other passage, a suicide note from a woman whose husband divorced her, an event which was followed by the death of her little daughter.

This is the tenth night I've sat in this empty room holding this little bottle of sleeping pills. Why don't I swallow them? Why do I write all this down? Because I want to talk—I need to talk! I wish I felt better like I did when Jim and I divorced. Then it was just anger and disappointment. Yes, that's how it was then. Whatever the pain of it, I didn't expect it to last. That's the important part. I could cry then; I can't cry now. When Penny died, everyone said, "You're taking it so well. You're wonderful! So brave! *Isn't that a laugh?* Complimenting me for being a Zombie! Suicide has an ugly sound. They'll say I was immature, insane or hostile. I just ache. It isn't a dull ache, it's a roaring active pain—tossing and turning at my insides, digging and clawing at my body until I feel trapped into a tight corner, and there's no escape. To me, grief is not an emotion or a bruise. Grief is a monster who wraps you in straps of steel, twisting them ever tighter about your body until you scream in anguish, but it is all invisible. You are invisible. And so alone. And time crawls by and your pain increases until you are desperate to end the agony. And before you know it, you've found the sleeping pills, and for a moment you're almost free—just thinking that quiet sleep will kill the pain once and for all. And yet, you hesitate. I'm afraid to die. Why am I so afraid? But I'm more afraid to live. . . . (Words found beside the body and empty bottle.)

When we start into a downward spiral such as this we need to remember St. Paul's admonition, "Put on the whole armor of God . . . that you may stand in the evil day!" In this case we need the breastplate of the protection of the people of God, those who can incarnate for us the truth that God remains faithful to us even when we lose our capacity to act in our own enlightened self-interest and the interests of those who love us.

And as a community, as Christians, we need to be sensitive to those who might not be able to remember to act and call us. If we hear the kinds of words in the note above, or get inklings from actions and behaviors of the kind of realities underlying those words, we need to go into action, get into the fray, intercept those processes, interrupt the cycle, interject first stability then encouragement. It may sound heavy or clumsy-footed in this sophisticated age, but there is a passionate, directive side to Christian existence and God definitely doesn't want any child of his to be bushwhacked by any of life's harsh unexpected events, and he *calls us* to carry that message of positive affirmation in an embodied flesh and blood manner.

We must leave our phone number in a prominent place with those terrorized by grief and help them to promise to contact us if the going gets too rough, and get them to commit themselves to a direction for their life for at least the next day or some specified period of time. We must risk being or looking foolish if need be as we fumble around trying to instill or allow them to borrow from us the will to *struggle* and the awareness that if they *hang on* we'll be able to look back on any experience and reap the benefits of its message to our total life.

Not long ago, I had a close friend who was a judge. Never did I see him show or express any feeling. But his mother died and he asked me to do a graveside service. In the meantime, his wife phoned me and said: "It would mean a lot to Don if you would sing this old hymn his mother loved, but he's afraid to ask you." Now I've never had a choir director ask me to sing solos. In fact, just the other day, two darling Methodists were outside my office while I was shaking the rafters singing a magnificent number and remarked at my peak crescendo: "O my gosh, the preacher is singing again," and closed the door. But you know, as I croaked and emoted through that old song with full confidence in my art, that sober judge wept uncontrollably. And I know what you are thinking now. But my serious point in relating that story is: You don't have to be any great shakes with another during mourning.

The idea is to start the siphoning off of the inner feelings they can't deal with for some reason, the draining away of the dregs of hurt. When we are sad, we think we want to withdraw into a hole sometimes, when what we need at that time is companionship—someone who can interrupt inactivity with a pot of tea or cookie, an invitation to lunch, a helping arm in cleaning the house or doing the dishes, sometimes someone with a willingness to sit with us and look over old pictures and listen to stories of what we remember and miss, to pray with us, or perhaps simply go for a walk with us in the woods, be there and never say a thing. But whether a person can express what he or she needs or we can guess or whether we can deliver appropriately, the greatest grace that lay or professional helpers eventually become aware of is that God can use us all to do a lot of good, even if it is *in spite of ourselves.* So whether we feel qualified or adequate or not, let's take heed from the wisdom and directives of Luther, and go ahead and risk "sinning bravely." One person, one good visit, one experience can ease years of heartache.

The "mourning period" may be kind of a quiet period of recuperation and changing of priorities if all goes its natural course. It is one cut above the first shock, paralysis, and sense of helplessness. The complications that arise are neither unusual nor sinful. It can be sinful, however, if those who love us allow us to continue to suffer beyond what is necessary. And sometimes those who care for us must observe our grief and tell us whether our degree of suffering seems unwittingly self-inflicted or our unhappiness self-enlarged. It can be convenient to malinger sometimes and convenient for those around us not to notice. But friendships that do credit to the name can embrace whatever embarrassment or discomfort is needed to speak the truth in love and get things on honest, fertile ground.

The period of recovery, is a slow regaining of the capacity to participate in a strange different world with a growing desire to reinvest in the markets of life, to continue living to the fullest the life the lost loved one cared for so much. There is a growing sense of new discoveries of personal capabilities, of a willingness to harvest new joys that might be different than old ones which can still be remembered and valued with satisfaction and thanksgiving.

If we have been open to living the deepest realities of our being during the mourning process and if the community has blessed us with its support and affirmation of our movement, we discover a new openness and trust in human relationships, human possibilities. Our horizon widens along with the options we have within that horizon. We have learned the comforting lesson that our flexibilities and capabilities have great substance. We latch onto every little spark of spirit which ignites within us. We encourage every little tingle of the will-to-do and the will-to-be and believe that these are signs from God.

In general, we recover as we strengthen our relationship with God by "letting him have his way in our lives," by "living by faith," by allowing ourselves to experience and go through the realities that we come to with the support of the greater community. The opposite of this would be a process of separating ourselves from God, the community, and our own creation; an attempt to be our own god and *control* our life by recreating things more to our own desires; not allowing feelings we do have, trying to manufacture ones we don't, holding on to old memories, not welcoming in the old ones which could be new, and keeping others out of our life who do not fit into old definitions of who they should be and what they should provide.

But if things progress fortuitiously in the natural, organic manner, we might even learn the sense of the Scripture which says, "Cast your cares upon the Lord for he careth for you," or of Jesus' words, "In this world you will have tribulation . . . but be of good cheer." Both Isaiah and Jesus had faith in the basic nature and potential of the "children of God." Each of us is fashioned to endure and overcome shock, mourning, and recovery. It is the function of friends, the church, and professional counselors to help us move through these stages. And *it is God's will for us.* Out of love we are created, from the richness of love we are sustained, and into the infinity of love, someday, each of us shall graduate beyond the reach of any sorrow or grief! Amen.

ON TALKING BACK TO GOD
Wayne E. Oates, Th.D.

A pioneer in the field who has published numerous aids for pastors, Wayne Oates needs no introduction for those familiar with pastoral care. He is currently Professor of Psychiatry and Behavioral Science at the University of Louisville School of Medicine after many years as Professor of Psychology of Religion at the Southern Baptist Theological Seminary.

His sermon *On Talking Back to God* deals with honesty in prayer life. It is a good example of speaking directly from within a community's faith stance and communicating a number of pastorally and psychologically important insights in a much more effective manner than if a more academic, meta-viewpoint stance had been employed (a stance many pastors are seduced into taking after so many years of academic training).

In a rural community of which I was pastor, a mother of twins told of hearing her sons say their prayers. One twin prayed earnestly: "Lord, have mercy on my brother here. He can't even milk a cow!" Before he could go further, the other twin interrupted and said: "Lord, it's not so! I milked half a bucket full and you know it!"

One does not know whether to laugh or not at such a story. Should little children be taught or permitted to be that frank with God in their prayers? Should we rebuke them and ask them to be on their best manners when they pray? Or should we know that in being this frank with God they are accepted by God in a special way of loving because they share their real feelings with God? My belief is that God does love them and any human beings who tell their real feelings to God in prayer. We cannot by keeping our real feelings to ourselves add to God's knowledge of us. We can only deepen our fellowship with God by doing so. In turn, God lovingly hears even our most negative prayers.

142

In the face of at least four different stresses or demands of life, we become resentful of our situation or have to deny that we are resentful. When we deny that we are resentful, we are likely to become too sweet for those around us to think we are real or too pious for those around us to put up with us comfortably. These four conditions are:

1. When we are expected to make a radical change in our way of life in order to grow up and put away childish things.
2. When we are expected to carry more responsibility than we think any one human being should be asked to carry.
3. When we think that we are totally alone in life, often after the loss of someone or some group of persons whom we consider very dear to us.
4. When some basic need of ours for food, for love, for the right to parenthood, for a place of leadership is frustrated and seemingly permanently denied.

The real question is: Can we say to God that we really don't like the way God is dealing with us? Can we express our resentments to God in prayer? I say that we can safely do so, that God expects us to tell things as they are in our prayers. In doing so we are accepted by God, just as we are, without one plea. Yet, if we do not express our displeasure to God directly, we do not open ourselves to God's power to enable us to make radical changes in our way of life. We fail to discover those around us who can share our too-heavy responsibilities with us. We fall back into self-pity over our gripes, grudges, and griefs. We live in the false expectation that life is to be without frustration of any kind. The main loss, however, is a kind of prayer life with our God who is not too far away, pious, or good for human nature's daily food.

The story we have read from Numbers presents this contrast. The children of Israel express their complaints to one another and to Moses. They did not express them to the Lord. They did not realize that by doing this they did not keep secrets from God. God heard them anyway. God was angry and displeased. They complained that they did not have meat. In the long run God gave them meat for a whole month "until it was coming out of their nostrils." Even our desires and cravings have their limitations.

This is a strange reminder of the Greek myth of Midas who was so greedy for gold that his fondest wish was granted, but everything he touched turned to gold until he discovered that there were persons and values he cherished more than gold. The real danger of greedy prayers is that they will be answered, full measure, pressed down, shaken together and running over.

By contrast, Moses expressed his feelings of injustice and his frustrations with the childishness of the Israelites directly to God. He challenged God's wisdom: "Why hast thou dealt ill with thy servant? And why have I not found favor in thy sight, that thou dost lay the burden of all this people upon me: 'Carry them in your bosom, as a nurse the suckling child, to the land which thou didst swear to their fathers'? Where am I to get meat to give to all this people? For they weep before me and say: 'Give us meat, that we may eat.' I am not able to carry this people alone; the burden is too heavy for me. If thou wilt deal with me thus, kill me at once, if I find favor in thy sight, that I may not see my wretchedness."

God affirmed Moses in his direct expression of his feelings to God as God. He was rewarded for "talking back to God." God rewarded him with the help of seventy elders as Moses confessed that he could not carry the burdens all alone. God rewarded him with real growth as a leader. Moses grew into the wisdom that he was not alone in his struggles. More than all this, God rewarded Moses with a deeper fellowship with God as God. God did not expect Moses to be limitless. God said: "I will come down and talk with you there; and I will take some of the spirit which is upon you and put it upon them; and they shall bear the burden of the people with you, that you may not bear it yourself alone."

Thus, it takes courage to express our displeasures, complaints, feelings of injustice, frustration and hopelessness to God directly. Such courage is rewarded with the goodness of God. God has not given us a spirit of fear, but of power, love, and self-control. God expects us to approach the throne of grace boldly and with confidence, that we may find mercy and receive grace to help in time of need. In Jesus Christ God has come down to meet us at the level of everyday's most desperate concern and to hear our most desperate and negative concern directly.

Yet, we have been programmed differently. We tend to take the tiny little slide picture of our relationship to our parents and blow it up on a large screen. We tend to think about God the way we do in some patterns of child rearing. One particular pattern of child rearing sounds like this:

> The parent says to the child: "I don't want any of your back talk. Hush! I will mellow your mouth with my fist. Do as I say because I say so. If you so much as open your mouth to me, I will beat you to a pulp."

Thus we tend to think about God. We think God will be hotly displeased with us if we "talk back" to God. We will be destroyed. We are supposed to knuckle under and say that everything that happens is God's will and never to be questioned, especially in our prayers to God. We can grumble among ourselves or to each other, but we can never pour out our complaints to God.

Already I hope you are beginning to talk back to me in your mind. You might say: "Oh, no! I could never do that. I have to accept everything without question. You can never question God." If you are talking back to me, I am glad. You have a right to question me. I have tried to imagine what your questions would be. As I do so, I can think of two.

First, does the rest of Scripture, especially the New Testament, validate the assumption that we can talk back to God? My answer is: Let's take a look. Hannah was unable to have children. She felt the reproach of her neighbors and the denial of the favor of God. Even Eli the priest thought she was drunk when she was "pouring out her complaint to God." She was rewarded by God for telling God of her excruciating frustration.

Ezekiel came face to face with God. He fell on his face in fear. God said to him: "Stand up on your feet, that I may talk with you." Psalm 22 says:

> My God, my God, why hast thou forsaken me?
> Why art thou so far from helping me,
> from the words of my groaning?
> O my God, I cry by day, but thou doest not answer;

and by night, but find no rest.
But I am a worm, and no man;
scorned by men, and despised by the people.
He committed his cause to the Lord;
let him deliver him, let him rescue him,
for he delights in him!
I am poured out like water,
and all my bones are out of joint;
my heart is like wax,
it is melted within my breast.
The Lord is my shepherd.
My strength is dried up like a potsherd,
and my tongue cleaves to my jaws;
thou dost lay me in the dust of death.
But thou, O Lord, be not far off!
O thou my help, hasten to my aid!

In the New Testament, Nathaniel spoke sneeringly of Jesus, asking: "What good thing can come out of Nazareth?" When Jesus met him, he said: "Behold is a man in whom there is no guile." He complimented him on his transparentness even with his most negative feelings. What a relief Nathaniel must have been in contrast to persons who like the Pharisees tried to trap him, match wits with him, or to say one thing to him while trying to hide another. Yet the writer of the Fourth Gospel portrays Jesus as a discerner of the hearts of men and women because he knew already. We cannot, as Jacob Boehme has said, add to God's knowledge of us by conveying our inmost thought. We can only be enriched by a deeper fellowship with God.

So, in both the Old and New Testaments, we find that talking back to God is a reality to be reckoned with in any accurate appreciation of biblical faith in God.

A second question you have the right to ask is: "So what? Say that it is O.K. with God for us to challenge God with our inmost thoughts. What then? What good does that do?"

It does a lot of good. First, if we tell God these things first, we will find that we will have told our inmost thoughts to someone who loves us and understands us better than even we ourselves do. When we speak of these things to others later, we do so with more wisdom. It is one thing to tell other people what we think. It is another to tell people things we have not thought through. Expressing our darkest thoughts to God in prayer has a way of making us think them through and enabling us to receive from God his revelation to us of what we really do think.

Second, telling God exactly how we feel enables us to have done with the idolatry of our hurts, our frustrations, our gripes, our grudges, and our griefs.

Never do we see this more clearly than when we are faced with the loss of someone by death, divorce, or just plain abandonment. We ask of God: "Why?" "Why me?" "Why did you take my loved one?" At their heart, such questions often point to our worship of the dead, our nursing of a grudge, our preference for isolation from other people, our subtle need to control others by an unassuageable grief. When we refuse to come to terms with events such as death, etc., over which we no longer have any control, then we push ourselves into the vain expectation of ourselves that we *be* a god.

In short, we encounter God as the God of the living and not the dead, and as one who is a living God, not one who dies, leaves or abandons us. We cannot expect to have any lasting city in a changing, fluctuating world. The things that can be shaken have been shaken for us in order that the things that cannot be shaken may remain.

Finally, telling it like it is to God puts us in fellowship with God so that our fears are allayed and our questions about and questionings of God can be answered at the source. Thus, prayer becomes more down-to-earth and real. The disciples by the seaside had this experience with the resurrected Lord Jesus Christ. He startled and frightened them, Luke tells us (24:36). He encouraged them to observe closely his feet and hands and see that he was flesh and blood. Luke tells us that they still "disbelieved for joy" and wondered as they ate broiled fish with him. Talking back to God results in a prayer life of "disbelief for joy."

The invitation of the Old Testament to "talk back to God" is found in Isaiah 1:18:

Come now, let us reason together, says the Lord; though your sins are as scarlet, they shall be as white as snow. Though they are red like crimson, they shall become as wool.

The invitation of the New Testament is found in Revelation 3:20:

Behold I stand at the door and knock. If anyone will hear my voice and open the door and let me in, I will come in and eat with that one and that one with me.

Postscript

A PRAYER LETTER TO GOD
Archie Smith, Jr. Ph.D.

In *A Prayer Letter to God* Archie Smith (see biographical note preceding *The Church's Ministry in a Lonely World*) takes a creative risk in using a different imaginative and personalized form for expressing a congregation's thanksgiving, confession, petition and intercession on a Sunday morning. While offering the congregation's concerns in prayer and praise in a particular way, the letter also illustrates Oates' value of honesty in prayer as well as a number of other values and concerns expressed explicitly or implicitly throughout the volume. The prayer letter was used October 18, 1982 at the McGee Avenue Baptist Church, Berkeley, California where Smith and his family are members and where Smith is often involved in leading the Sunday morning liturgy.

Dear God:

Hi! You probably are not getting much mail these days. We are all so busy living our lives, pursuing our goals, worrying about the economy, the possibility of nuclear war, and wondering about what the president is really saying that we don't take time to talk with you about what we're doing with our lives or to acknowledge that you are interested in us. I guess you must feel a bit ignored.

I thought I would write a prayer letter to you rather than to pray in the usual way we go about it. I want to share what is on my mind and to open my life and our lives to you in some new ways. I just want to talk. First of all, I want to say thanks for the beautiful and unusual fall weather we've been having. These extra days of warm sun are a reminder of the surprise of creation, of your warmth, care and constant love for us. A lot of us have been enjoying these warm days working around the house on weekends, trips to the beach, watching the turning of the leaves, time spent in solitude, sharing these warm fall days with family or a special friend. Thanks for these days of uncommon beauty.

There is also a lot of loneliness, some disappointments, hurt, pain and uncertainty here, too. Some of us have questions about the future: "Where do we go from here?" Some of us have aches and pains in our body—the doctors can't find the causes, let alone the solution. And so, we have come to this place with a fair amount of anxiety and uncertainty—a "not knowing." There is a lot of sadness and failing health here. There is some tension in our Church family as well as some excitement about deepening our Christian witness.

I know you are concerned about these things too. But somehow it feels important to acknowledge them to you openly, and to ask you to help us to responsibly share one another's burdens. We do not always do so with compassion. We do not always talk about what is important to us. We are often afraid to trust; and we are not always sure whom we can trust.

We are not always straight with you or with each other about what really matters. We are hardly straight with ourselves. We hide because we fear being known. And we sometimes think that if other persons really got to know us, they won't like what they see.

They may even talk about us behind our back. But you know us—and that is a bit scary too. It is easier to write you off by saying you don't exist. But it would cut us deeply if someone were to write us off or even to deny our existence. It somehow seems safer to hide in our fear than to be known as we really are. So, help us to bear one another's burdens, and so fulfill the law of Christ.

We also fear you. We fear that you will ask us to embrace challenges and struggles that we would rather ignore such as seeking solidarity with refugees, displaced persons, the incarcerated and many others who are oppressed by our power expressed through our government in places like South Africa, El Salvador, Nicaragua, the Near East, or closer to home in the barrios and ghettos of our own community.

Right now we seem preoccupied, even confused by both sides of the nuclear arms race. We hardly know where to stand. We hear false assurances of peace, but we are not at peace. How can we be at peace in a world which seems to grow more precarious each day and pushes toward nuclear catastrophe? We even hear assurances from those we've elected to responsible leadership positions—assurances that we can actually survive a nuclear war. War is much on our minds and in our intentions and pretentions.

I imagine that you too must be alarmed by all this, especially by our rhetoric, egoism and self-deception and seeming willingness to risk obliterating your creation on earth.

But what can we do, God? We face a problem unprecedented in previous generations. We seem not to have learned very much about peace-making from the tragedies of Hiroshima, Nagasaki, and the horrors of the Nazi concentration camps of Europe.

Can you help us gain our sanity, sense of justice and responsibility for the whole world—and not just our segment of it? Some of us fail even to acknowledge that we have a problem of stupefying proportions. We seem willing even to engage in pointless discussions of whether or not there will be postal delivery after nuclear rockets have done their destructive work. And so we look to you for help and hope. We rejoice wherever your Spirit of truth breaks through the hardness of our hearts and your love dissolves the tears that have imprisoned us. Help us to take the mask from the face of life that we may see the dim arches of your providence looming above the concerns of our day; your wondrous glory hidden in the turning furrows of time; the image of your hope in all people struggling to do your will; your strength made manifest in the meek and lowly of this world. We need your help. We need a comprehensive vision of justice and mercy to guide and liberate us from our limited views of the future. This real possibility of nuclear catastrophe somehow seems connected with our problems of loneliness. It is not all clear to me or to us just how it is connected, but I sometimes wonder if our deep sense of loneliness and lack of trust in one another and in you has caused us to withdraw from engagement in sharing the inner regions of ourselves, our deepest feelings and convictions. We also withdraw from the pain of others. We have enough of our own troubles to worry about, we say. Our dialogue is monologue. We can't see taking on the woes of others beyond our own family and professional commitments. There is not enough time, and the problems of the community or world are too complex and confounding, we tell ourselves.

It is hard to be a person for others. And it is hard for them to be for us. But we really do need your help—your spirit which calls us forward and frees us to love people more than we love things.

I know this letter is getting awfully long and I don't want to end it on a pleading note. Perhaps others of us will write you a letter too. But I just want to say in closing: Thanks for listening and thanks for all the rich experiences we have had in our lives to inspire us. Thanks for growth that comes from suffering. Thanks for music, for the cool refreshing sensation of water on a hot day, for fresh fruit, for renewed friendships, for forgiveness, for the refreshing rain that waters the earth and makes living things grow. And thanks for being present even when we turn our backs on you in anger, indifference or out of ignorance or ingratitude and fear. Above all, help us to embrace life in its fullness—both joy and pain, our laughter and our tears, our life as well as our death and rebirth. Reveal to us the joy and freedom made available in Jesus, the Christ. Help us to witness to the power of his resurrection in the activity of our lives.

Thanks for listening. Goodbye for now.